T0164928

# ANGER,

## A BIBLICAL PERSPECTIVE

D.E. GILLASPIE

WestBow
PRESS
A DIVISION OF THOMAS NELSON

WestBow Press books may be ordered through booksellers or by contacting:

WestBow Press
A Division of Thomas Nelson
1663 Liberty Drive
Bloomington, IN 47403
www.westbowpress.com
1-(866) 928-1240

Because of the dynamic nature of the Internet, any web addresses or links contained in this book may have changed since publication and may no longer be valid. The views expressed in this work are solely those of the author and do not necessarily reflect the views of the publisher, and the publisher hereby disclaims any responsibility for them.

Certain stock imagery © Thinkstock.
Any people depicted in stock imagery provided by Thinkstock are models, and such images are being used for illustrative purposes only.

ISBN: 978-1-4497-2509-9 (e)
ISBN: 978-1-4497-2510-5 (sc)
ISBN: 978-1-4497-2511-2 (hc)

Library of Congress Control Number: 2011916413

Printed in the United States of America

WestBow Press rev. date: 9/9/2011

I would like to thank my wife Brenda for her patience during the long hours of alienation while I was researching and writing this book. I want to thank my Pastor, Bishop Richard Campbell, for reviewing and editing this material. Many thanks go out to my church family for their input and help along the way. Mostly I want to praise and thank my Lord God Almighty for His inspiration and guidance.

# CONTENTS

# INTRODUCTION

Anger has been part of my life as long as I can remember. My father was quick to anger no matter how small the provocation. I believe it was because of his military experience. Some battle hardened men never learned to leave the battlefield. The war was over, but the families paid the price.

On a cold winter day in 1968, the Lord Jesus Christ got a hold of me and put my feet on that straight and narrow path. I did not realize the full implication at the time. Following my fleshly man, whom I had not totally crucified, I followed the footsteps of my earthly father, and let every little thing provoke me to anger. Being a proud man, I joined the United States Marine Corps in 1971. Talk about a group of angry people!! I guess that's the result of being trained to break things and kill people.

The first thing I did when I began this study was to sit down and list all the things that made me angry. When I opened the Bible and began to read the "anger" verses, it didn't take me long to realize that it was not about me. The first lesson I learned is that we learn about ourselves through prayer and the study and seeking of God and His ways. Didn't Jesus tell us this? "But seek ye first the kingdom of God, and his righteousness; and all these things shall be added unto you." (Matthew 6:33)

There came a day when something interrupted my plans and disrupted my 'orderly' life. I immediately became angry! My sweet wife spoke to me at that time and my anger turned into rage. Since I needed to go to the store anyway, I said something insulting and left the house. I was in a huff and alone. I cooled off enough to feel the conviction of God and had an urge to study the Bible to see what it had to say about the subject. Little did I realize that there are 947 verses dealing with the anger and its variations? God must consider this subject pretty important to have included so many references to it in His Word.

This study is entirely Bible based. I prayed and fasted and let the Holy Spirit lead me. I used very few references, commentaries, or analyses. I wanted this lesson to come straight from God. This is as I learned it.

I ask you to read this prayerfully and study the verses yourself. God has no respect of persons. He will teach you with the same amount of delight as He did me.

# INTRODUCTION TO ANGER

Anger is natural part of all of us. It became part of humanity when Adam fell from grace and was kicked out of paradise. In one way or another we have been trying to get back into or recreate paradise in our own way ever since. Paul states that in time past we "were by nature the children of wrath..." (Ephesians 2:3) He then admonishes us to, "Be ye angry, and sin not..." (Ephesians 4:26). Jesus, Himself got angry (Mark 3:5). Therefore, we can conclude that anger is not a sin, but how you respond to it or express it can be.

There are different degrees of anger. Webster's Dictionary defines anger as a feeling of displeasure resulting from injury, mistreatment, opposition, etc. and usually shows itself in a desire to fight back at the supposed cause of this feeling; <u>anger</u> is broadly applicable to feelings of resentful or revengeful displeasure; <u>indignation</u> implies righteous anger aroused by what seems unjust, mean or insulting; <u>rage</u> suggest a violent outburst of anger in which self-control is lost: <u>fury</u> implies a frenzied rage which borders on madness; <u>wrath</u> implies deep indignation expressing itself in a desire to punish or get revenge. <u>Wroth</u> (adj.) is to be twisted with anger, wrathful, incensed; <u>displease</u> or <u>displeased</u> is failure to please or be pleased, to be disagreeable, annoy, offend, irritate. All these terms are used in reference to anger. This could refer either God's anger or man's anger. I've listed them here for reference purposes.

Anger can be good or bad depending on your response as was stated earlier. The downside of anger is obvious. It is the main cause of fights and, by extension, wars. Anger turned inward on oneself produces drug and alcohol abuse. When turned on loved ones you get divorce, domestic violence and abuse. When turned on others we see attitudes that make you not care what hurtful things you say or do, or who sees or hears you. Destruction of property or even loss of life is not uncommon. You can lose your job, hurt your pets or other animals just for spite. It will isolate you from those you need the most at that time, your 'support group' – family and friends. How many times have we heard angry people or even said ourselves, "Leave me alone!" CAUTION: Anger opens our lives to Satan. It gives him a door big enough to drive an 18-wheeler through. Again I reference Ephesians 4:26, 27, "Be ye angry, and sin not: let not the sun go down upon your wrath: Neither give place to the devil."

There is, however, an upside to anger. A parent who is not angry (displeased) will not discipline their children when they misbehave or are in danger. This also can be taken too far. "... provoke not your children...", Ephesians 6:4; Colossians 3:21. Without some degree of anger you will not protect you family, home or property. Anger can also strengthen your resolve to accomplish some task that you are having trouble with and aid in success. The most proper anger is in defense of our LORD and His scriptures. We call this "righteous indignation." You will never sin if your anger is because you are defending God.

Again Paul writes in Ephesians 4:31 "Let all bitterness, and wrath, and anger, and clamor, and railing, be put away from you with all malice." Bitterness is the settled disposition of one who is resentful. Anger is strong, sudden antagonism, explosive, potential murder. Wrath is like roaring furnace, settled indignation. Clamor is yelling at others. Railing is "blasphemy" in the Greek, meaning "speaking against God or man." Malice takes delight in inflicting hurt or injury. Such conditions of the inward life as that indicated by the prohibitions listed here are the bane of earthly existence. What incredible waste and loss of all that is precious flow out of the undisciplined lives of unrepentant people; and, tragic as that is, it must be held even more deplorable that many Christians have never learned to live above the behavior Paul listed in this powerful verse. Anger and wrath are bad, but malice is worse, because it is more rooted and deliberate; it is anger heightened and settled. I'm not saying that anger is a good characteristic or a good lifestyle. Just that there are two sides to everything, one for good to the glory of God and the other to sin and destruction.

Anger is the cause and origin of a great deal of sin, and exposes us to the curse of God, and his judgment (Matthew 5:22). We should always, in the expressions of our enthusiasm, be careful to distinguish between the sinner and the sin, so as not to love nor bless the sin for the sake of the person, nor to hate nor curse the person for the sake of the sin.

No one can know the mind of God! But, you can know the thoughts of God by knowing what makes Him angry. If you know what makes Him angry, then you can live in a manner to avoid these. This is just another way of saying, "Live by the Spirit, not by flesh." A phenomenon occurred during this research! Instead of getting angrier, I received a deep peace and calmness.

I have divided the scriptures by:
1. The things that anger God
2. The things that angered the people of the Bible
3. The Psalm that deals with anger
4. The Proverbs that deals with anger

I have listed all the verses in a separate chapter at the back of this book. I recommend that you prayerfully read and study them yourself to achieve maximum benefit.

You will notice that there are a lot of references to the Old Testament. Some people will say that since we are in the New Testament age that these verses have nothing to do with us. Paul explains in Romans 3:31 "Do we then make void the law through faith? God forbid: yea, we establish the law." Simply put, the New Testament builds on the foundation of the Old Testament. "All scripture is given by inspiration of God, and is profitable for doctrine, for reproof, for correction, for instruction in righteousness" (2 Timothy 3:16).

I pray that everyone who reads this book will be blessed with the peace and understanding that I have received and anger in any of its forms will be removed from your life. I pray that all who read this will, also, be able to recognize and control their anger until it is totally removed by our blessed Lord and Savior Jesus Christ. Amen and Amen.

# WHAT MAKES GOD ANGRY

Do you think of God as a loving benevolent grandfather? Will He forgive and forget no matter what? Will He say, as we hear so many earthly grandfathers, "Kids will be kids?" While God does love us, as His creations, we have free will. That means we have the choice to obey Him or ignore Him.

God definitely is kind and repays (rewards) the obedient believer with more than he or she deserves. However, never be fooled into believing that God does not get mad! There came a time when God became so mad He killed His only Son to destroy sin and unrighteousness. Of course, this was for our benefit, to convert the human creation from sinful and lost beings to righteous children of God. Thank you God!!

You would think that God would get angry at sin and those who disobey the 'Ten Commandments' (Exodus 20), while this is true; there are 51 reasons for God's anger mentioned in the Scriptures. These are identified and expounded upon in the body of this chapter. In the interest of brevity, I have chosen the most descriptive and direct verses to make the point. I encourage you to follow up and study all the verses. I've listed them in the back of this book.

## Cruelty -

The first thing mentioned in the Scriptures that makes God angry is murder (cruelty). The commandment against murder (cruelty) is not given until Exodus 20:13. Jacob curses Simeon and Levi because they became so angry they killed the men of Shalem in the land of Canaan (Genesis 33:18; 49:5-7). This is how they avenged the honor of their sister, Dinah (Genesis 34:25,26). There was no law at this time; therefore, they were not guilty of murder. They were only accused of cruelty. Jacob cursed his sons with separation one from another (Genesis 49:7). However, the curse of separation did not come to pass until they were in the land that God gave the Israelites. When it was divided, the tribes of Levi and Simeon were not located near each other.

## Idolatry -

The commandments (Exodus 20:2-17) were written on the stone tablets. "And the LORD said unto Moses, Come up to me into the mount, and be there: and I will give thee tables of stone, and a law, and commandments which I have written; that thou mayest teach them." (Exodus 24:12) The people disobeyed them before Moses could bring the law of God to the people from off the mountain (Exodus 32:7-19). The people had Aaron make them a golden calf (Exodus 32:1-6). God did not show Himself in any form to the Israelites when He spoke to them at Horeb. He only allowed them to hear His voice (Deuteronomy 4:11-20). If He would have presented Himself in any form, the people probably would have made an image of that form and, thereby, had a legitimate reason to practice idolatry. God did not want anything to come between Him and His chosen people. Any needs, concerns, disagreements or complaints were to be taken directly to the priests at the tabernacle (later to the temple). There are many other places in the Bible where

Israel failed to abide by God's covenant. They are referred to as "doing evil in the sight of the LORD thy God" (Deuteronomy 4:25). The punishment of disobedience is the loss of property and home, and to be taken captive into strange surroundings where they would be forced to worship idols and false gods (Deuteronomy 4:25-28). God promised delivery, if they would seek Him (Deuteronomy 4:29-31). The promise is for us today as evidenced by the use of the phrase "the latter days." Since the relationship of God and His chosen people are likened to husband and wife, the Bible refers to worshiping other gods as "whoring." When the children of Israel turned to other gods and away from the only true God, He brought to pass the curse He promised. He sent them into bondage (2 Kings 17:7-24). He brought many nations against them over the generations. In this passage He uses Assyria (2 Kings 17:24). The LORD gave them many opportunities and sent many warnings to them to repent and be saved (2 Kings 17:13), yet they ignored the prophets and seers. This is a perfect example how God will make a way of escape (1 Corinthians 10:13). Idolatry will separate you from God (Ezekiel 14:5). Temporarily at first, then slowly the item or focus of your affection will totally remove your attention from Him. You do not need statues of the gods of other nations. Your idol can be in your heart, it does not have to be physical thing (Ezekiel 14:3, 4). Any distraction that keeps you from God for an extended period of time is an idol. If your job is not going well or your home life is rocky or you're in jeopardy of losing it or there are many distractions keeping you away from church, Bible reading, your daily prayer or days of fasting, check your priorities. You have probably have created an idol somewhere in your life. You may not even be aware of it. Problems in your life are the symptoms; the fault is in the lack of focus on God and too much focus on daily life and its pleasures. Be careful that God does not become angry with you!

## Hardness of heart –

God gets angry at the hardness of man's heart (Deuteronomy 29:19, 20). This condition is also referred to as being 'stiff-necked'. The man with a hard heart will read or hear God's word, then say or think to him, "that was a good sermon or interesting Bible story, but it was not for me. I don't have that problem or it does not relate to my life." Or even, "that was for the people back then. It does not apply today." The LORD takes this so serious that He will utterly destroy that person.

"Ye stand this day all of you before the LORD your God; your captains of your tribes, your elders, and your officers, with all the men of Israel, Your little ones, your wives, and thy stranger that is in thy camp, from the hewer of thy wood unto the drawer of thy water: That thou shouldest enter into covenant with the LORD thy God, and into his oath, which the LORD thy God maketh with thee this day: That he may establish thee today for a people unto himself, and that he may be unto thee a God, as he hath said unto thee, and as he hath sworn unto thy fathers, to Abraham, to Isaac, and to Jacob. Neither with you only do I make this covenant and this oath; But with him that standeth here with us this day before the LORD our God, and also with him that is not here with us this day (For ye know how we have dwelt in the land of Egypt; and how we came through the nations which ye passed by; And ye have seen their abominations, and their idols, wood and stone, silver and gold, which were among them:) Lest there should be among you man, or woman, or family, or tribe, whose heart turneth away this day from the LORD our God, to go and serve the gods of these nations; lest there should be among you a root that beareth gall and wormwood; And it come to pass, when he heareth the words of this curse, that he bless himself in his heart, saying, I shall have peace, though I walk in the imagination of mine heart, to add drunkenness to thirst: The LORD will not spare him, but then the anger of the LORD and his jealousy shall smoke against that man, and all the curses that are written in this book shall lie upon him, and the LORD shall blot out his name from under heaven." (Deuteronomy 29:10-20) Jesus came across a man with a withered hand in the synagogue early in His ministry. Knowing the elders were watching Him close for any offense of the Mosaic Law, He asks them if doing well on the Sabbath was acceptable with their law. Jesus healed the man, but was grieved because He knew their hearts were hard and blind because of their hatred of Him (Mark 3:1-5). Hardening your heart against the covenant and laws of God and being unrepentant will only make the anger of God fiercer against you on judgment day. Hardness of heart will definitely keep you out of heaven (Hebrews 3:7-19).

## Attempting to destroy God's anointed people -

Attempting to destroy God's anointed people will get you on the wrong side of God quickly. He will protect His people from all harm. He protects the king, "For the king trusteth in the LORD, and through the mercy of the most High he shall not be moved. Thine hand shall find out all thine enemies: thy right hand shall find out those that hate thee. Thou shalt make them as a fiery oven in the time of thine anger: the LORD shall swallow them up in his wrath, and the fire shall devour them. Their fruit shalt thou destroy from the earth, and their seed from among the children of men. For they intended evil against thee: they imagined a mischievous device, which they are not able to perform. Therefore shalt thou make them turn their back, when thou shalt make ready thine arrows upon thy strings against the face of them." (Psalms 21:7-12) He will protect His people from invading armies, "Thou didst march through the land in indignation, thou didst thresh the heathen in anger. Thou wentest forth for the salvation of thy people, even for salvation with thine anointed; thou woundedst the head out of the house of the

wicked, by discovering the foundation unto the neck. Selah."
(Habakkuk 3:13). God will take care of His people and keep them
from harm. "...Touch not mine anointed, and do my prophets no
harm." (Psalms 105:15)

## Doubting God's ability to sustain His people –

One of the earliest complaints from the Israelites was that they
were going to die in the desert, they had no food. In other words,
God could not sustain them. They often cried, "...Wherefore have
ye brought us up out of Egypt to die in the wilderness? for there
is no bread, neither is there any water..." (Numbers 21:5). After
wandering in the desert for forty years, being fed and their clothes
not getting old and rotting off their bodies, not to mention seeing
the great works and miracles God had performed in their sight, the
people still did not trust God to defeat the armies of the nations
who occupied the land He was giving them (Deuteronomy 1:29-
36). Where God takes you He will supply all your need. "But my
God shall supply all your need according to his riches in glory by
Christ Jesus." (Philippians 4:19)

## God's people's iniquities –

God is angered by His people's iniquities which are exposed
by the light of God's countenance (Psalms 90:8). As God's people,
we are supposed to be different from the world. If we do the same
thing the sinners do, we are no different than they. God speaks
to Ezekiel and lays out a list of charges against Jerusalem. These
being: they made idols to defile themselves, the leaders abused
their power and sold their favors, the people brought dishonor
upon their fathers and mothers, they oppressed the stranger in
their midst, they vexed the fatherless and the widow, "Thou
hast despised mine holy things, and hast profaned my Sabbaths."
(Ezekiel 22:8), they committed slander (literally they sold their
lies to do harm to the innocent), they sacrificed to idols and other

gods, they committed lewdness, "they have taken gifts to shed blood, thou hast taken usury and increase, and thou hast greedily gained of thy neighbors by extortion, and hast forgotten me, saith the LORD God." (Ezekiel 22:1-12) You are the only evidence of God some people see. If you do not live by the laws of God and commit iniquities (sin against God), then those people will see no advantage to taking Jesus as their personal Savior. Because you are not any better in your way of life than they are! They will have no reason to feel a personal conviction. They can always say that they are doing no more than you are and you consider yourself saved. We already know that willful sinning separates us from God. It also makes us a reproach and mocks our beliefs to the unbeliever and the wicked. "...because for our sins, and for the iniquities of our fathers, Jerusalem and thy people are become a reproach to all that are about us." (Daniel 9:16)

## Sinners -

Sinners, as expected make God angry. For this discussion, we will define sinners as those who would not accept or serve God no matter how much proof is given or how convinced they are they need a higher power in their life. These people just will not accept God. Isaiah 13 describes the judgment of the sinner. While these verses refer to directly to Babylon and her king, they are also a warning to all who reject the LORD. "They come from a far country, from the end of heaven, even the LORD, and the weapons of his indignation, to destroy the whole land. Howl ye; for the day of the LORD is at hand; it shall come as a destruction from the Almighty. Therefore shall all hands be faint, and every man's heart shall melt: And they shall be afraid: pangs and sorrows shall take hold of them; they shall be in pain as a woman that travaileth: they shall be amazed one at another; their faces shall be as flames. Behold, the day of the LORD cometh, cruel both with wrath and fierce anger, to lay the land desolate: and he shall destroy the sinners thereof out of it. For the stars of heaven and the constellations thereof shall not give their light: the sun shall be darkened in his going forth, and the moon shall not cause her light to shine. And I will punish the world for their evil, and the wicked for their iniquity; and I will cause the arrogancy of the proud to cease, and will lay low the haughtiness of the terrible. I will make a man more precious than fine gold; even a man than the golden wedge of Ophir. Therefore I will shake the heavens, and the earth shall remove out of her place, in the wrath of the LORD of hosts, and in the day of his fierce anger. And it shall be as the chased roe, and as a sheep that no man taketh up: they shall every man turn to his own people, and flee every one into his own land. Every one that is found shall be thrust through; and every one that is joined unto them shall fall by the sword. Their children also shall be dashed to pieces before their eyes; their houses shall be spoiled, and their wives ravished. Behold, I will stir up the Medes against them, which shall not regard silver; and as for gold, they shall not delight in it. Their bows also shall dash the young men to pieces; and they shall have no pity on the fruit of the womb; their eye shall not spare children. And Babylon, the glory of kingdoms, the beauty of the Chaldees' excellency, shall be as when God overthrew Sodom and Gomorrah. It shall never be inhabited, neither shall it be dwelt in from generation to generation: neither shall the Arabian pitch tent there; neither shall the shepherds make their fold there. But wild beasts of the desert shall lie there; and their houses shall be full of doleful creatures; and owls shall dwell there, and satyrs shall dance there. And the wild beasts of the islands shall cry in their desolate houses, and dragons in their pleasant palaces: and her time is near to come, and her days shall not be prolonged." (Isaiah 13:5-22) Their end shall be utter destruction. God says He will make men more scarce than gold. Their salvation cannot be bought. The people He will send to destroy them will not care anything for gold or silver. They will be ruthless, killing man, woman and child. They will also destroy land and buildings, leaving the area as desolate as Sodom and Gomorrah, uninhabited except for wild animals. Can you think of a better reason to accept Jesus Christ as your personal savior?

## When God's people get full, comfortable and forget God -

Israel had lived in peace and prospered. They attributed their wealth to the work of their own hands (Deuteronomy 8:17). The LORD had even warned His people about becoming complacent (Deuteronomy 6:1-12) God's people had gotten satisfied and comfortable in their situation and forget God (Hosea 13:6). All the things we have comes from God (Deuteronomy 2:7). We may have to work hard for the money to purchase what we need or desire, but it is God that gives us the strength and position that supplies the financing. This generation has it so easy! We get our food at a grocery store already processed. Our meat is slaughtered for us, packaged and cleaned so we have no need to hunt or raise animals for food. If we have gardens, they are hobbies and are to save us money. We really have no need of them. It is so easy for us to become comfortable and forget that God has provided all our sustenance. Watch yourself and be aware of your attitude! Do not forget to thank the LORD daily for what He has given us. If at any time you forget, God has provided for us a prayer for redemption. "Take with you words, and turn to the LORD: say unto him, Take away all iniquity, and receive us graciously: so will we render the calves of our lips." (Hosea 14:2) A little clarification is required here. One of the purposes of the sacrificing of the calf in the temple was as a praise offering, therefore verbal praise is called here '... the calves of our lips." Thank God daily and praise Him often. He is our provider, "Behold, he smote the rock, that the waters gushed out, and the streams overflowed; can he give bread also? can he provide flesh for his people?" (Psalms 78:20)

The family is so important to God that any separation between members causes an ache in God's heart. Jesus taught that if anyone has a grievance with a family member they should get that situation taken care of before they offer anything to God (Matthew 5:22-24). Jacob and Esau were twin sons of Isaac. Esau was considered the oldest. The birthright and inheritance was his. As the story goes, he was a hunter and one day he came home empty. Hunting all day made him hungry and he was without prey. He ask Jacob for some of his food and Jacob took advantage of his brother and sold him food for Esau's birthright. Esau never forgave Jacob. He passed his hate to his children. All his days, even to the present, are the decedents of Esau carrying hate for the decedents of Jacob. When God lead the Israelites into the Promised Land, He instructed them to go around Edom. This was the land of Esau's children. The Edomites never attacked Israel directly, but when they were carried into captivity, they would follow and pick off the weak and stragglers. This violated God's law. "Thus saith the LORD; For three transgressions of Gaza, and for four, I will not turn away the punishment thereof; because they carried away captive the whole captivity, to deliver them up to Edom: But I will send a fire on the wall of Gaza, which shall devour the palaces thereof: And I will cut off the inhabitant from Ashdod, and him that holdeth the sceptre from Ashkelon, and I will turn mine hand against Ekron: and the remnant of the Philistines shall perish, saith the LORD God. Thus saith the LORD; For three transgressions of Tyrus, and for four, I will not turn away the punishment thereof; because they delivered up the whole captivity to Edom, and remembered not the brotherly covenant: But I will send a fire on the wall of Tyrus, which shall devour the palaces thereof. Thus saith the LORD; For three transgressions of Edom, and for four, I will not turn away the punishment thereof; because he did pursue his brother with the sword, and did cast off all pity, and his anger did tear perpetually, and he kept his wrath forever:" (Amos 1:6-11)

## Doubting God's ability to use you as you are -

Moses talked to God and never doubted that He was God. When God told him what He wanted Moses to do, Moses then doubted that he could perform the task. He made all kinds of excuses why he was unable or not qualified to obey God. God had already qualified him before He contacted Moses. God became angry with the many excuses he made. "And Moses said unto the LORD, O my Lord, I am not eloquent, neither heretofore, nor since thou hast spoken unto thy servant: but I am slow of speech, and of a slow tongue. And the LORD said unto him, Who hath made man's mouth? or who maketh the dumb, or deaf, or the seeing, or the blind? have not I the LORD? Now therefore go, and I will be with thy mouth, and teach thee what thou shalt say. And he said, O my Lord, send, I pray thee, by the hand of him whom thou wilt send. And the anger of the LORD was kindled against Moses..." (Exodus 4:10-14). Doubting God's ability to use you in your present condition when you are called will anger our LORD every time. Your doubt essentially calls Him a liar. You are saying that God does not have the power to transform you into what you need to be! He has chosen you and prepared you for the job at hand. We see ourselves as we are at that moment in time, weak, untested and unlearned. God sees you as He will make you and in the position to which He calls you.

## Complaining -

God had delivered the Israelites from Egypt and bondage. He had brought them across the harsh desert. They were supplied with everything they needed for their journey, food, their clothes and sandals that did not get old or rot apart, yet they were not satisfied. Manna, the food of angels, was not good enough for them! They wanted meat! So, in their discontentment and as people of the flesh, they complained. "And when the people complained, it displeased the LORD: and the LORD heard it; and his anger was kindled..." (Numbers 11:1) The Hebrew translation of "...it displeased the LORD..." actual is closer to "...it was evil in the ears of the LORD..." We must be careful not to anger God by complaining. Paul instructs us to, "do all things without murmurings and disputings (Philippians 2:14). Even the military and work ethics teaches to do a disagreeable task or serve an undeserved punishment then register your complaint to your supervisor. God takes complaining against His chosen people very serious. There came a time when the Levites thought they ought to do more and have more responsibility in the service of the tabernacle. They complained against Moses and Aaron. God desired to kill them, Moses prayed for them and stopped their punishment. However, the leaders of the rebellion and 250 followers were swallowed up by the earth (Numbers 16:1-35). The rest of the camp saw what had happened to the Levites, and perceiving them to be Holy because of their duties to the tabernacle, they were scared and complained to Moses saying, "Ye have killed the people of the LORD." (Numbers 16:41) This so angered God He sent a plague into the congregation. Aaron had to make an atonement for them to stop the plague (Numbers 16:46-48). It should be evident now that God takes complaining very, very serious. Therefore, we better take it serious too!!

## Mutiny, speaking against God's chosen ones or authority –

Miriam convinced Aaron that they were just as important as Moses (Numbers 12:2). Actually their displeasure with Moses stemmed from prejudice. He had married an Ethiopian woman. He had married outside the Israelite nation (Numbers 12:1). God was so angry at this that he made Miriam a leper and caused her to stay outside the camp for seven days (Numbers 12:10-14). We saw in a previous paragraph that God deals harshly with those who speak against His chosen ones.

## Israel mixing with the nation they were to displace –

The people of Israel were called to be a separated people (Deuteronomy 7:6). God's chosen. Somehow they never understood that. During the journey to the "land flowing with milk and honey" they rested a while in Shittim. Forgetting God quickly, they began to worship other gods and idols. We learned earlier how God feels about idolatry. Unlike the time they had Aaron make them an idol (the golden calf), they were persuaded to turn from God by the people who lived in that region (Numbers 25:1-13). When God lead Israel into the "land flowing with milk and honey" the armies were told to destroy all the things pertaining to the nation that occupied the land at that time. Men, women, children, and animals they were not to leave one thing, not to make treaties or intermarry with them. They were to be utterly destroyed (Deuteronomy 7:2,3,5). God said that any people left in the land would lead Israel away from God to idols ((Deuteronomy 7:4). Once you turn your life over to God, you must separate yourself from sinful things and people. Any contact with the past lifestyle will be a temptation and the people will try to draw you back. No matter how hard you try to keep yourself from returning to the old ways, you will always slip and have to ask God for forgiveness. Remember we have an advocate with the Father, Jesus Christ.

## Doubting God can deliver on His promises –

Doubting God can deliver on His promises reveals a lack of faith and calls God a liar, again. Moses lead the Israelites to the border of the promised land. God had promised to clear out the inhabitants. Moses sent spies to survey the land and the situation. Seeing through man's eyes and forgetting the word of God, the spies returned with a fearful report. They said the land was indeed good and rich (Numbers 13:26,27), but the inhabitants were giants and mighty men, too strong to be conquered (Numbers 13:28,29,31). When God took the people out of Egypt, He promised that they would be given a land they did not build on that was flowing with "milk and honey." The spies were so afraid of the people of the land, they took their minds off of God and lied about the condition of the land. They called it "a land that eateth up the inhabitants" (Numbers 13:32). God's anger burned against the people and He made them wander in the wilderness for forty years (Numbers 32:13). When God says He will do something, there is no doubt that He can do it. After all, we're talking about the creator of the universe!

## People who would lead Israel away from God –

The Israelites moved into the promised land and started to conquer the inhabitants and saw they had kings over them. The Israelites were jealous and wanted a king over them too. Those who would be put in charge would range from the very godly to those who would pervert God's laws and people. God really became angry at those people who would lead Israel away from God to idols. Jeroboam was not the first, but his story illustrates the point. He built two golden calves and had them distributed in the country. He put one in Bethel and the other in Dan. Totally opposite ends of the country! The LORD had put His house (temple) in Jerusalem. All of the people were instructed to go there to sacrifice and worship. Jeroboam decided that the people could just as easily go to one of the two cities where he put the calves, and not have to travel all the way to Jerusalem (1 Kings 12:25-33). Some people took advantage of the closer sites! This of course, is idolatry. Remember what God thinks about idolatry?! God sent a prophet to the alter at Bethel and pronounced judgment upon it. He found Jeroboam there performing sacrifices. When

Jeroboam heard the judgment against his alter, he tried to arrest the man of God, He dried up Jeroboam's hand (1 Kings 13:1-5). There are many examples of the kings leading Israel away from God. Just a few, for example, there's Baasha (1 Kings 16:1-33), Ahab (1 Kings 21:17-27), Ahaziah (1 Kings 22:51-53) and Joash (2 Kings 13:2,3).

## Disobedience –

God calls us to be a peculiar people, separated to God and obedient to His laws and ordinances. "And be not conformed to this world: but be ye transformed by the renewing of your mind, that ye may prove what is that good, and acceptable, and perfect, will of God." (Romans 12:2) When we are obedient to Him, we receive blessings and power beyond our wildest imaginations. "But as it is written, eye hath not seen, nor ear heard, neither have entered into the heart of man, the things which God hath prepared for them that love him." (1 Corinthians 2:9) Is this not the state in which we want to continually exist? Closely walking and talking with God daily! If we do not continually stay in contact with God we can disobey Him even unintentionally or innocently. David, the great man of God, wanted to bring the ark of God to Jerusalem. It belonged in the temple which was at Jerusalem. Uzzah was struck dead for touching the ark when it was on its journey towards the city, a sad incident, which damped the merry spirit of the crowd, stopped the progress of the ark, and for the present, dispersed this great assembly which had come together to attend and celebrate it, and sent them home very frightened (2 Samuel 6:1-11). Uzzah's offense seems very small. He and his brother Ahio, the sons of Abinadab, in whose house the ark had long been lodged, had been used to attending it. To show their willingness to prefer the public benefit to their own private honor and advantage, undertook to drive the cart in which the ark was carried. This was probably the last service they were likely to perform for it, others would be charged with its care when it arrived in Jerusalem and was put in its rightful place. Ahio lead the cart, to clear the way, and if needed, to lead the oxen. Uzzah followed close to the side of the cart. It happened that the oxen shook it (2 Samuel 6:6). By some accident or other the ark was in danger of being overthrown. Uzzah, thereupon, laid hold of it to save it from falling, we have reason to think he had a very good intention, to preserve the reputation of the ark and to prevent a bad omen. Yet this was his crime. Uzzah was a Levite! Priests were the only people allowed to touch the ark. The law was definite concerning the Kohathites, that, though they were to carry the ark by the staves, yet they must not touch any holy thing, lest they die (Numbers 4:15). Uzzah's long familiarity with the ark, and the constant attendance he had given to it, might have caused his presumption, but would not excuse it. His punishment for this offense seems very great (2 Samuel 6:7). The anger of the LORD was kindled against him (for in sacred things he is a jealous God) and he smote him there for his rashness, as the word is, and struck him dead upon the spot. There he sinned, and there he died, by the ark of God, even the mercy-seat would not save him. Why was God severe with him? First, the touching of the ark was forbidden to the Levites expressly under pain of death — lest they die; and God, by this instance of severity, would show how he might justly have dealt with Adam and Eve, when they had eaten that which was forbidden under the same penalty— lest you die. Secondly, God saw the presumption and irreverence of Uzzah's heart. Perhaps he wanted to show, before this great assembly, how confident he was with the ark, having been so long acquainted with it. Familiarity, even with that which is most sacred, is apt to breed contempt. David afterword's confessed that Uzzah died for an error they were all guilty of, which was carrying the ark in a cart. Because it was not carried on the Kohathites' shoulders, the LORD made that breach upon us (1

Chronicles. 15:13). But Uzzah was singled out to be made an example, perhaps because he had been most insistent in advising that way of transportation. However, he had fallen into another 'innocent error', which was created by that one. Perhaps the ark was not covered, as it should have been, with the covering of badgers' skins (Numbers 4:6), and that was a further provocation (1 Chronicles 13:10). Disobedience, as innocent and unintended as it might be, bears grave consequences. Willful disobedience is just as serious to God and carries just as severe penalty. When Israel willfully disobeyed, God sent their enemies against them, to destroy them and carried the remnant into captivity. He also, sent pestilence to destroy them and scattered them to the four corners of the earth (Ezekiel 5:5-14). Yet another example would be when Moses struck the rock instead of speaking to it as God had commanded (Numbers 20:7-13). There are many more examples of the children of Israel, God's chosen people, willfully disobeying Him. You will find them listed in the back of this book. Moses gave a beautiful prophetic exhortation (a warning) to obey God. "And it shall come to pass, if ye shall hearken diligently unto my commandments which I command you this day, to love the LORD your God, and to serve him with all your heart and with all your soul, that I will give you the rain of your land in his due season, the first rain and the latter rain, that thou mayest gather in thy corn, and thy wine, and thine oil. And I will send grass in thy fields for thy cattle, that thou mayest eat and be full. Take heed to yourselves, that your heart be not deceived, and ye turn aside, and serve other gods, and worship them; and then the LORD's wrath be kindled against you, and he shut up the heaven, that there be no rain, and that the land yield not her fruit; and lest ye perish quickly from off the good land which the LORD giveth you." (Deuteronomy 11:13-17) Let this warning be engraved into your mind and heart. Fear God and never turn away to disobedience and sin. Remember the consequences are severe. "For the wages of sin is death; but the gift of God is eternal life through Jesus Christ our LORD". (Romans 6:23)

## Pride –

Pride really gets God angry. Almost as much as idolatry. There are many verses in the Bible that warn us and teach against it. This is Satan's sin! He was the head angel until he thought himself to be as important as God (Ezekiel 28:12-19). Then he went from being 'Lucifer' (the Day Star; bringer of light) to Satan (the adversary; accuser). "How art thou fallen from heaven, O Lucifer, son of the morning! how art thou cut down to the ground, which didst weaken the nations! For thou hast said in thine heart, I will ascend into heaven, I will exalt my throne above the stars of God: I will sit also upon the mount of the congregation, in the sides of the north: I will ascend above the heights of the clouds; I will be like the most High." (Isaiah 14:12-14)

Assyria surrounded Jerusalem ready for battle. Their king Sennacharib taunted the inhabitants of Judah to break their spirits and create an easy defeat. Hezekiah assured his people, that God would fight on their side (2 Chronicles 32:7,8). The Jews fortified their city in anticipation of the attack. No attack came! God had sent His angel to fight for them. Sennacherib returned home defeated because the angel of the LORD had killed "...all the mighty men of valor, and the leaders and captains in the camp of the king of Assyria."(2 Chronicles 32:21) Hezekiah assumed his preparation had scarred Sennacherib off. He was so proud that his preparedness had saved the city. He did not thank God or offer sacrifices of thanksgiving (2 Chronicles 32:25). Some of the citizens did though (2 Chronicles 32:23). Pride can make you think things are owed to you, therefore the kindness you receive you will not repay. Ephraim, was a proud nation, it was so proud, that they were even proud that they were proud! (Isaiah 28:1-4) Are you proud? Watch out!!

## Turning away from God (backsliding) -

"Ah sinful nation, a people laden with iniquity, a seed of evildoers, children that are corrupters: they have forsaken the LORD, they have provoked the Holy One of Israel unto anger, they are gone away backward." (Isaiah 1:4) Those who do not know the LORD cannot be 'backsliders.' You cannot turn away from a person, place or situation where you have never been or whom you have never known. We study His word, attend church and worship Him, and witness to others because we love Him. If as 'good Christians', we believe that we know God, then why does the LORD ask, "...who is blind as he that is perfect, and blind as the LORD'S servant? Seeing many things, but thou observest not; opening the ears, but he hearest not." (Isaiah 42:19,20) God has called us to be His people. To serve Him and obey Him. The responsibilities and cares of this life can slowly come between us and our Savior if we are not careful. It starts slow and innocent at first. We come home after a hard day on the job, lay on the couch to rest, wake up when it's time for bed and neglect to read the Bible or pray. Let's say you leave your house to go to church and the car does not start, so you miss church. How about when the children or you are sick. No sin here, we all get sick. But if you are sick, where better to be than in church where you can get healed? The little things pile up until you are just staying home from church and the Bible gets dusty because you never even pick it up. It is not God that causes you to backslide, it is a trick of the devil. As was stated earlier in this chapter, anything that comes between you and God in an idol. When we 'serve' idols, we run the risk of making God angry. "For my people have committed two evils; they have forsaken me the fountain of living waters, and hewed them out cisterns, broken cisterns, that can hold no water." (Jeremiah 2:13) God refers to turning away from Him as 'evil'. "...broken cisterns, that can hold no water" refers to idols, false gods or anything that take precedents over God. If you stay home to watch the 'big game' or do anything that is not of God... WATCH OUT! Our LORD tries and tries to call the backslider to return to Him. Some will return, but some will come half-heartily. "I hearkened and heard, but they spake not aright: no man repented him of his wickedness, saying, What have I done? every one turned to his course, as the horse rusheth into the battle." (Jeremiah 8:6) The most complete warning and exhortation to the backslider can be found in Jeremiah, chapters 7 and chapter 8:5-19.

## Those who despise the Word of God –

You can lack understanding of the word of God or know the word and be disobedient. These things will displease God and He will teach you or correct you through the Holy Spirit. Those who despise the word of God will anger Him to the point of bringing His judgment and wrath upon them. "And the LORD God of their fathers sent to them by his messengers, rising up betimes, and sending; because he had compassion on his people, and on his dwelling place: But they mocked the messengers of God, and despised his words, and misused his prophets, until the wrath of the LORD arose against his people, till there was no remedy." (2 Chronicles 36:15,16). Again He says, "Woe unto them that call evil good, and good evil; that put darkness for light, and light for darkness; that put bitter for sweet, and sweet for bitter! Woe unto them that are wise in their own eyes, and prudent in their own sight! Woe unto them that are mighty to drink wine, and men of strength to mingle strong drink: Which justify the wicked for reward, and take away the righteousness of the righteous from him! Therefore as the fire devoureth the stubble, and the flame consumeth the chaff, so their root shall be as rottenness, and their blossom shall go up as dust: because they have cast away the law of the LORD of hosts, and despised the word of the Holy One of Israel. Therefore is the anger of the LORD kindled against his people, and he hath stretched forth his hand against them, and hath smitten them: and the hills did tremble, and their carcases were torn in the midst of the streets. For all this his anger is not turned away, but his hand is stretched out still." (Isaiah.5:20-25) When you despise the Word, you become a law unto yourself. The ways you like you consider good and the ways you dislike or the people that try to correct you, you will condemn as evil. Thus, society will be thrown into chaos. It does not matter whether they are believers of God or not! Right is right and wrong is wrong. Paul wrote concerning this, "For when the Gentiles, which have not the law, do by nature the things contained in the law, these, having not the law, are a law unto themselves..." (Romans 2:14)

## Pride mixed with arrogance -

"An high look, and a proud heart, and the plowing of the wicked, is sin." (Proverbs 21:4) Pride mixed with arrogance makes you believe you know better how things should be done. It doesn't matter if you are at church or at work. You are smarter than all those around you and you have the perfect answer for any situation, no matter how experienced your companions and co-workers are. This makes God very angry. "The LORD sent a word into Jacob, and it hath lighted upon Israel. And all the people shall know, even Ephraim and the inhabitant of Samaria, that say in the pride and stoutness of heart, The bricks are fallen down, but we will build with hewn stones: the sycamores are cut down, but we will change them into cedars. Therefore the LORD shall set up the adversaries of Rezin against him, and join his enemies together; the Syrians before, and the Philistines behind; and they shall devour Israel with open mouth. For all this his anger is not turned away, but his hand is stretched out still." ( Isaiah 9:8-12) God had given definite instructions on what materials were to be used in construction. The people decided they knew how to rebuild even stronger. To change things for the better, hand cut stones in lieu of bricks and cedar for the wood instead of sycamore (Isaiah 9:10). Another example of God's judgment upon the proud and arrogant is the judgment of Assyria (Isaiah 10:12-19). God had used Assyria to punish Israel of her idolatry. The king of Assyria became confident in his own ability and strength of his armies. God promised their destruction (Isaiah 10:16-19). It is not uncommon for God to use nations to bring punishment upon Israel then when the time of the punishment was over, to bring punishment to the nation He used. He did create the whole world and all nations are under His control. As the old spiritual says, 'He has the whole world in His hands.'

## Hypocrites –

God, Himself, gives us the definition of a hypocrite. "Wherefore the LORD said, Forasmuch as this people draw near me with their mouth, and with their lips do honour me, but have removed their heart far from me, and their fear toward me is taught by the precept of men" (Isaiah 29:13) Jesus stated it in this manner, "Ye hypocrites, well did Esaias prophesy of you, saying, This people draweth nigh unto me with their mouth, and honoureth me with their lips; but their heart is far from me. But in vain they do worship me, teaching for doctrines the commandments of men." (Matthew 15:7-9) When our LORD defines a condition and calls attention to it in both the Old Testament and the New Testament, I figure it is of great importance. Even though God had protected Israel and fought their enemies for them, they did not follow Him. "For the people turneth not unto him that smiteth them, neither do they seek the LORD of hosts. Therefore the LORD will cut off from Israel head and tail, branch and rush, in one day. The ancient and honourable, he is the head; and the prophet that teacheth lies, he is the tail. For the leaders of this people cause them to err; and they that are led of them are destroyed. Therefore the LORD shall have no joy in their young men, neither shall have mercy on their fatherless and widows: for every one is an hypocrite and an evildoer, and every mouth speaketh folly. For all this his anger is not turned away, but his hand is stretched out still." (Isaiah 9:13-17) God used Assyria to punish His people for their hypocrisy. "O Assyrian, the rod of mine anger, and the staff in their hand is mine indignation. I will send him against an hypocritical nation, and against the people of my wrath will I give him a charge, to take the spoil, and to take the prey, and to tread them down like the mire of the streets." (Isaiah 10:5,6) Job describes the state of the hypocrite. "...the hypocrite's hope shall perish: whose hope shall be cut off, and whose trust shall be a spider's web." (Job 8:13,14) No hypocrite will stand in God's presence (Job 13:16). The hypocrite's joy is short lived (Job 20:5). There is no hope for the hypocrite when God takes away his soul (Job 27:8). A hypocrite will collect the wrath of God against himself, will be hard hearted when the LORD tries to correct him and he will die young (Job 36:13,14). "...the congregation of hypocrites shall be desolate, and fire shall consume the tabernacles of bribery. They conceive mischief, and bring forth vanity, and their belly prepareth deceit."(Job 15:34,35). When your leaders are hypocrites, society will be corrupted. "That the hypocrite reign not, lest the people be ensnared." (Job 34:30) You can see why worshiping God with all your heart, mind and soul is so important. You can also understand why hypocrisy makes God angry. Those who will live righteous are promised God's protection. "He that walketh righteously, and speaketh uprightly; he that despiseth the gain of oppressions, that shaketh his hands from holding of bribes, that stoppeth his ears from hearing of blood, and shutteth his eyes from seeing evil; he shall dwell on high: his place of defence shall be the munitions of rocks: bread shall be given him; his waters shall be sure." (Isaiah 33:15, 16) Jesus admonished the scribes and Pharisees of their hypocrisy. I'm sure it did not make them happy to be scolded in public. But

Jesus came to save the whole world, not just the poor and lowly. This event is recorded in Matthew 23:2-7,13-31. You can read for yourself. I believe it will have more of an impact that way. Hypocrites make up their own rules (1 Timothy 4:1-5). They are taught man's doctrine, not God's. Therefore, they kind of make it up as they go hoping God will see the good in their hearts and look favorably upon their good intentions. We all must obey God's laws! It should be easy, Jesus only gave us two. "And thou shalt love the LORD thy God with all thy heart, and with all thy soul, and with all thy mind, and with all thy strength: this is the first commandment. And the second is like, namely this, Thou shalt love thy neighbour as thyself. There is none other commandment greater than these." (Mark 12:30,31) We cannot 'pick and choose.' With God it's all or nothing. He does, however, give us plenty of chances to repent and turn to Him. My favorite call to return to God is found in 2 Chronicles 7:14, "If my people, which are called by my name, shall humble themselves, and pray, and seek my face, and turn from their wicked ways; then will I hear from heaven, and will forgive their sin, and will heal their land." Thank you, precious, gracious, merciful God!!

## Wickedness (the wicked) -

It should be no surprise that God's anger and wrath is kindled at wickedness and the wicked. Wickedness is best defined in scripture. "...but we have done wickedly: neither have our kings, our princes, our priests, nor our fathers, kept thy law, nor hearkened unto thy commandments and thy testimonies, wherewith thou didst testify against them. For they have not served thee in their kingdom, and in thy great goodness that thou gavest them, and in the large and fat land which thou gavest before them, neither turned they from their wicked works." (Nehemiah 9:33-35) The results of wicked living is also, best described in scripture. "Behold, we are servants this day, and for the land that thou gavest unto our fathers to eat the fruit thereof and the good thereof, behold, we are servants in it: and it yieldeth much increase unto the kings whom thou hast set over us because of our sins: also they have dominion over our bodies, and over our cattle, at their pleasure, and we are in great distress. And because of all this we make a sure covenant, and write it; and our princes, Levites, and priests, seal unto it." (Nehemiah 9:36-38) Doesn't this sound a lot like what we, as Americans, are experiencing in this day and age? Consider this: the Israelites were given the land (their inheritance) not because they were the chosen, even though that was part of it, but because of the wickedness of the nations that occupied the land (Deuteronomy 9:4,5). Could we be losing our inheritance because of our wickedness? God prescribed a severe penalty for the man or woman who would commit wickedness in the midst of the Israelites. They were to be taken and stoned to death! (Deuteronomy 17:2-5) Why such a severe penalty? Wickedness will spread like fire and all the people will be affected (Isaiah 9:18-21). God hides His face from the wicked (Jeremiah 33:4,5). Wickedness does not go unnoticed by God (Jonah 1:2). The LORD notices the sinning person even though He does not take immediate action (Job 10:14-16). This is another example of God's mercy. Wanting all men to be saved, and giving every opportunity for the sinner to turn to Him for salvation, He will exercise great patience. The judgment of the LORD will be painful upon the wicked and complete and swift (Jeremiah 30:23,24). Thank God for His mercy and grace! Without it where would we be?

## Those who decree unrighteous decrees (who make unfair and unjust laws) –

It cannot be stated better than the scriptures put it, "Woe unto them that decree unrighteous decrees, and that write grievousness which they have prescribed; to turn aside the needy from judgment, and to take away the right from the poor of my people, that widows may be their prey, and that they may rob the fatherless! And what will ye do in the day of visitation, and in the desolation which shall come from far? to whom will ye flee for help? and where will ye leave your glory? Without me they shall bow down under the prisoners, and they shall fall under the slain. For all this his anger is not turned away, but his hand is stretched out still." (Isaiah 10:1-4) Those who are in a position to make laws that affect God's people better take extreme care as to the consequences of those laws. God will not take lightly the oppressions, injustices or unrighteousness of any man made laws. POLITICIANS BEWARE!! God is real whether you believe in Him or not!

## Rebellious people –

God's righteous anger is kindled by rebellious people, those who have not turned away from Him completely, but do not trust on Him fully either. The whole chapter of Isaiah 30 describes God's curse for the rebellious and blessings for those who return to Him. "Woe to the rebellious children, saith the LORD, that take counsel, but not of me; and that cover with a covering, but not of my spirit, that they may add sin to sin" (Isaiah 30:1) God describes them as, "That this is a rebellious people, lying children, children that will not hear the law of the LORD: which say to the seers, See not; and to the prophets, Prophesy not unto us right things, speak unto us smooth things, prophesy deceits: get you out of the way, turn aside out of the path, cause the Holy One of Israel to cease from before us." (Isaiah 30:9-11) These people still believe in God and know Him as the ultimate authority, but choose not to follow Him fully. The people of Judah had an army coming against them at this time. Instead of calling upon the LORD, their deliverer, they went to Egypt to hire mercenaries to save them. Isaiah prophesied, "For the Egyptians shall help in vain, and to no purpose: therefore have I cried concerning this, Their strength is to sit still." (Isaiah 30:7) God said that all the people had to do was to wait upon Him and He would take care of the problem. Isn't this a promise that we are all familiar with? "But they that wait upon the LORD shall renew their strength; they shall mount up with wings as eagles; they shall run, and not be weary; and they shall walk, and not faint." (Isaiah 40:31) Again God promises, "For thus saith the LORD God, the Holy One of Israel; In returning and rest shall ye be saved; in quietness and in confidence shall be your strength..." (Isaiah 30:15) We serve a patient and merciful God. He calls us to return to Him when we sin or fall away so many times in His word. But is this not the theme of the Holy Bible, the word of God? Our dear beloved, righteous Savior watching us fail so many times and providing us with a way back to Him. We have the choice! Come to Jesus and be saved or be a law unto ourselves and be lost for eternity. He is always waiting on us. "And therefore will the LORD wait, that he may be gracious unto you, and therefore will he be exalted, that he may have mercy upon you: for the LORD is a God of judgment: blessed are all they that wait for him. For the people shall dwell in Zion at Jerusalem: thou shalt weep no more: he will be very gracious unto thee at the voice of thy cry; when he shall hear it, he will answer thee. And though the LORD give you the bread of adversity, and the water of affliction, yet shall not thy teachers be removed into a corner any more, but thine eyes shall see thy teachers: and thine ears shall hear a word behind thee, saying, This is the way, walk ye in it, when ye turn to the right hand, and when ye turn to the left." (Isaiah 30:18-21) You can expect many blessings when you fully serve the LORD. Some listed in Isaiah are, "Then shall he give the rain of thy seed, that thou shalt sow the ground withal; and bread of the increase of the earth, and it shall be fat and plenteous: in that day shall thy cattle feed in large pastures. The oxen likewise and the young asses that ear the ground shall eat clean provender, which hath been winnowed with the shovel and with the fan. And there shall be upon every high mountain, and upon every high hill, rivers and streams of waters in the day of the great slaughter, when the towers fall. Moreover the light of the moon shall be as the light of the sun, and the light of the sun shall be sevenfold, as the light of seven days, in the day that the LORD bindeth up the breach of his people, and healeth the stroke of their wound." (Isaiah 30:23-26) "Ye shall have a song, as in the night when a holy solemnity is kept; and gladness of heart, as when one goeth with a pipe to come into the mountain of the LORD, to the mighty One of Israel." (Isaiah 30:29) The LORD also promised curses for those who choose to ignore His call. Since I pray that all who read this are or will be children of God, I will leave the reading and study of these passages to you. The whole story is told in Isaiah, chapter 30.

## False teaching and teachers –

Teachers of God's word are in a dangerous position. They are to teach the true word of God adding nothing nor subtracting anything. "For I testify unto every man that heareth the words of the prophecy of this book, If any man shall add unto these things, God shall add unto him the plagues that are written in this book: and if any man shall take away from the words of the book of this prophecy, God shall take away his part out of the book of life, and out of the holy city, and from the things which are written in this book." (Revelation 22:18,19) False teachers will be dealt with very harshly by our LORD. I encourage you all to make sure you know and understand the true way and real meaning of the scriptures before you attempt to teach others. Teachers and pastors are referred to as ' shepherds'. God has set them over us to care for and watch over us as you would care for sheep. There are many places in the Bible where the LORD referrers to His church as 'a flock'. Jeremiah 23:1-4 gives a word of warning to the negligent shepherds. The day is at hand when God will deal with them concerning the trust and charge given to them, "Woe be to the pastors..." (to the rulers, both in church and government) who should be to those they are set over as pastors to lead them, feed them (spiritually), protect them, and take care of them. They are not owners of the sheep. God calls them "the sheep of my pasture." Woe be to those who are commanded to feed God's people, and pretend to do it, but who, instead, scatter the flock, and drive them away by their violence and oppression, and have not visited them, nor taken any care for their welfare, nor concerned themselves at all to tend to them. In not visiting them, and doing their duty, they in effect scatter them and drove them away. The beasts of prey, also, scattered them. The shepherds, who should have kept them together, are to blame. Woe be to them when God will visit upon them the evil of their doings and deal with them as they deserve. They did not visit or tend the flock as was their duty, therefore, God will visit them in a way bringing vengeance. Then there is a word of comfort to the neglected sheep. Though the under-shepherds take no care of them, no pains with them, but betray them, the chief Shepherd will look after them. Though the interests of God's church in the world are neglected by those who should take care of them, and postponed to their own private secular interests, the church will still stand. God will perform his promise, even though those he employs do not perform their duty. Though there be but a remnant of God's flock left, a little remnant, that has narrowly escaped destruction, he will gather that remnant, will find them out wherever they are and find out ways and means to bring them back out of all countries where he had driven them (Jeremiah 23:3). It was the justice of God, for the sin of their shepherds, that dispersed them; but the mercy of God shall gather in the sheep, when the shepherds that betrayed them are cut off. They shall be brought to their former habitations, as sheep to their folds, and there they shall be fruitful, and increase in numbers. And, though their former shepherds took no care of them, they shall be re-established. If someone abused a sacred office, there is no reason it should be abolished. "And I will set up shepherds over them which shall feed them: and they shall fear no more, nor be dismayed, neither shall they be lacking..." (Jeremiah 23:4) Previously they were continually exposed and disturbed with one type of danger or another; but now they will no longer be in fear, nor be amazed or confused; they shall be in no danger from without, in no fright from within. Previously some of them were killed by the beasts of prey; but now none of them shall be lacking, none of them missing. Though the times may have been bad for quite a while with the congregation, those days are now over, there's a new shepherd in charge. We are warned by Peter that false prophets and teachers will be in the church in the latter days. "But there were false prophets also among the people, even as there shall be false teachers among you, who privily shall bring in damnable heresies, even denying the LORD that bought them, and bring upon themselves swift destruction." (2 Peter 2:1)

## False priests and prophets –

Those who the people should be able to rely and depend most on turned their back upon God and used their office for their own gain. False priests, prophets and princes saw opportunities for enlarging their own positions and fortunes. As always, the people saw what their leaders were doing and began behaving the same way. The priests and princes would devise an evil scheme and the prophets would lie and say that God said that the scheme was righteous or justified. When God sent true prophets to the people, the leaders would stir up the crowds against God's prophets and they would be killed by the people (Matthew 23:31,37). Thus the false leadership stayed intact and in power. The false prophet separated the people from God. "Which think to cause my people to forget my name by their dreams which they tell every man to his neighbor, as their fathers have forgotten my name for Baal." (Jeremiah 23:27) God calls to His people to return to Him and His ways. How many times have we seen this? "Thus saith the LORD of hosts, Hearken not unto the words of the prophets that prophesy unto you: they make you vain: they speak a vision of their own heart, and not out of the mouth of the LORD." (Jeremiah 23:16) Our LORD sees all, nothing is hid from Him. God knows all that those false prophets try to do. "I have not sent these prophets, yet they ran: I have not spoken to them, yet they prophesied. But if they had stood in my counsel, and had caused my people to hear my words, then they should have turned them from their evil way, and from the evil of their doings. Am I a God at hand, saith the LORD, and not a God afar off? Can any hide himself in secret places that I shall not see him? saith the LORD. Do not I fill heaven and earth? saith the LORD. I have heard what the prophets said, that prophesy lies in my name, saying, I have dreamed, I have dreamed. How long shall this be in the heart of the prophets that prophesy lies? yea, they are prophets of the deceit of their own heart..." (Jeremiah 23:21-26) The LORD is very much against the false prophets. Actually this should come as no surprise. "Therefore, behold, I am against the prophets, saith the LORD, that steal my words every one from his neighbor. Behold, I am against the prophets, saith the LORD, that use their tongues, and say, He saith. Behold, I am against them that prophesy false dreams, saith the LORD, and do tell them, and cause my people to err by their lies, and by their lightness; yet I sent them not, nor commanded them: therefore they shall not profit this people at all, saith the LORD. And when this people, or the prophet, or a priest, shall ask thee, saying, What is the burden of the LORD? thou shalt then say unto them, What burden? I will even forsake you, saith the LORD. And as for the prophet, and the priest, and the people, that shall say, The burden of the LORD, I will even punish that man and his house. Thus shall ye say every one to his neighbor, and every one to his brother, What hath the LORD answered? and, What hath the LORD spoken? And the burden of the LORD shall ye mention no more: for every man's word shall be his burden; for ye have perverted the words of the living God, of the LORD of hosts our God. Thus shalt thou say to the prophet, What hath the LORD answered thee? and, What hath the LORD spoken? But since ye say, The burden of the LORD; therefore thus saith the LORD; because ye say this word, The burden of the LORD, and I have sent unto you, saying, Ye shall not say, The burden of the LORD; Therefore, behold, I, even I, will utterly forget you, and I will forsake you, and the city that I gave you and your fathers, and cast you out of my presence: and I will bring an everlasting reproach upon you, and a perpetual shame, which shall not be forgotten." (Jeremiah 23:30-40) It is important to know that the word 'burden' here means message or oracle. (according to Unger's Bible Dictionary). "Therefore have I poured out mine indignation upon them; I have consumed them with the fire of my wrath: their own way have I recompensed upon their heads, saith the LORD God." (Ezekiel 22:31) All who live under false leadership will suffer, even the land itself. "And the word of the LORD came unto me, saying, Son of man, say unto her, Thou art the land that is not cleansed, nor rained upon in the day of indignation."(Ezekiel 22:23, 24) "For the land is full of adulterers; for because of swearing the land mourneth; the pleasant places of the wilderness are dried up, and their course is evil, and their force is not right." (Jeremiah 23:10) 'Swearing' here actually means cussing, according to Unger's Bible Dictionary. As we can easily see, it is better to live under God's direction and listen to His prophets than to be swayed by men who are only concerned with their own interests and fortunes. These men can ruin everything they touch! The only way to truly know what sort of people we have in charge of us is to study God's word and follow His direction.

## Those who rejoice in the misery of God's people -

God's anger and vengeance will fall hard on those who rejoice in the misery and punishment of God's people and take advantage of their situation. Israel has been surrounded by their enemies ever since they were lead out of bondage in Egypt. The countries of Ammon, Seir, Moab and Edom were relatives of Israel. Ammon, Seir and Moab were descendants of Lot. The Edommites were descendants of Esau, the brother of Jacob. These nations had a grudge against Israel. The dispute was perpetuated through the generations and was a great source of distress to the Israelites. These nations never directly attacked Israel, they joined with other nations to conquer them or followed behind picking off the weak and the stragglers. I believe the root cause of the hatred and aggression was basic jealousy. The children of Lot were jealous because God chose the children of Abraham instead of them. Likewise, Esau was angry with Jacob for stealing his birthright and blessing. He then taught his hatred to his descendants. The hatred of Israel by Ammon, Seir, Moab and Edom is disgusting to God. They are brothers that are locked in an eternal struggle for no real reason. God therefore, cannot possibly support the warring siblings and will punish them. To the Ammonites He says, "And say unto the Ammonites, Hear the word of the LORD God; Thus saith the LORD God; Because thou saidst, Aha, against my sanctuary, when it was profaned; and against the land of Israel, when it was desolate; and against the house of Judah, when they went into captivity; behold, therefore I will deliver thee to the men of the east for a possession, and they shall set their palaces in thee, and make their dwellings in thee: they shall eat thy fruit, and they shall drink thy milk. And I will make Rabbah a stable for camels, and the Ammonites a couching place for flocks: and ye shall know that I am the LORD. For thus saith the LORD God; Because thou hast clapped thine hands, and stamped with the feet, and rejoiced in heart with all thy despite against the land of Israel; behold, therefore I will stretch out mine hand upon thee, and will deliver thee for a spoil to the heathen; and I will cut thee off from the people, and I will cause thee to perish out of the countries: I will destroy thee; and thou shalt know that I am the LORD." (Ezekiel 25:3-7) To Seir and Moab He says, "Thus saith the LORD God; Because that Moab and Seir do say, Behold, the house of Judah is like unto all the heathen; therefore, behold, I will open the side of Moab from the cities, from his cities which are on his frontiers, the glory of the country, Bethjeshimoth, Baalmeon, and Kiriathaim, unto the men of the east with the Ammonites, and will give them in possession, that the Ammonites may not be remembered among the nations. And I will execute judgments upon Moab; and they shall know that I am the LORD." (Ezekiel 25:8-11) To the Edomites God says, "Thus saith the LORD God; Because that Edom hath dealt against the house of Judah by taking vengeance, and hath greatly offended, and revenged himself upon them; therefore thus saith the LORD God; I will also stretch out mine hand upon Edom, and will cut off man and beast from it; and I will make it desolate from Teman; and they of Dedan shall fall by the sword. And I will lay my vengeance upon Edom by the hand of my people Israel: and they shall do in Edom according to mine anger and according to my fury; and they shall know my vengeance, saith the LORD God." (Ezekiel 25:12-14) God punished Israel when they turned away from Him by driving them out of the land that He gave them. The exile was never permanent, He always sent a prophet to call them back. So for the surrounding countries to try to claim the land as their own could not be tolerated by God.

## Forsaking His commandments –

Today our LORD blesses us and secures our possessions and our lifestyle as long as we are following Him. When we turn from Him, He will allow something to happen and we will lose something, the longer we stay away the more we will lose. When we turn again to God, He will restore our blessings. They are never totally lost unless we become totally separated (by our choice) from God. Those who delight in the misfortunes and troubles of God's people will be dealt with just as harshly in this day and age as it was back then. This is just one reason why we must pray for and stand with Israel in her perils in this present time. We are created by and called to be God's people. To be truly a separate and holy people requires us to live by God's laws. Forsaking Him and living according to our own understanding is a sure way to incur God's wrath. He is with us always and as long as we obey He will help us through any situation we may get ourselves into. However, when we reach the point that we feel that we no longer need Him or our ideas are better than His and live according to our own laws forsaking Him, He will turn from us. "...Thus saith the LORD, Ye have forsaken me, and therefore have I also left you..." (2 Chronicles 12:5) Because the Israelites had turned away from God, He had delivered them into the hands of their enemies. He will never leave us completely. Nor will He ever repeal His promises. When He punished the Jews, He always left a 'remnant' to secure the land. Those taken into captivity would always have a place to return to and family there to remind them of the life they had when they kept God's commandments. "And now for a little space grace hath been showed from the LORD our God, to leave us a remnant to escape, and to give us a nail in his holy place, that our God may lighten our eyes, and give us a little reviving in our bondage." (Ezra 9:8) "...a little space..." means for a moment of time. God had shown grace to the Israelites by leaving some people behind to secure the land as belonging to God's chosen. 'Nail' is used here to indicate a permanent place holder similar to putting a pin in a map to mark a special place or point of interest. The nail is, of course, the remnant left behind. The LORD promised blessings for obeying His commandments. (Leviticus 26:3-12) Likewise, He warned of curses for disobedience. (Leviticus 26:14-39) You don't have to read the differences to realize that to be blessed is much better than to be cursed.

## Reneging on a vow (promise or pledge) -

God expects us to keep our promises. If we make a vow or pledge to God we are expected to pay or perform it. If there is the slightest doubt that you cannot fulfill the obligation, do not even open your mouth to make the vow. God will not accept the excuse that the pledge was made in error. "When thou vowest a vow unto God, defer not to pay it; for he hath no pleasure in fools: pay that which thou hast vowed. Better is it that thou shouldest not vow, than that thou shouldest vow and not pay. Suffer not thy mouth to cause thy flesh to sin; neither say thou before the angel, that it was an error: wherefore should God be angry at thy voice, and destroy the work of thine hands?" (Ecclesiastes 5:4-6)

## Afflictions of widows or of fatherless children -

Widows and orphans are especially close to the heart of God. He looks after them and cares for them with a jealous spirit. Do not be guilty of hurting one of God's wards. "Ye shall not afflict any widow, or fatherless child. If thou afflict them in any wise, and they cry at all unto me, I will surely hear their cry; and my wrath shall wax hot, and I will kill you with the sword; and your wives shall be widows, and your children fatherless." (Exodus 22:22-24) God makes special provisions for the widows and the fatherless, "When thou cuttest down thine harvest in thy field, and hast forgot a sheaf in the field, thou shalt not go again to fetch it: it shall be for the stranger, for the fatherless, and for the widow: that the LORD thy God may bless thee in all the work of thine hands. When thou beatest thine olive tree, thou shalt not go over the boughs again: it shall be for the stranger, for the fatherless, and for the widow. When thou gatherest the grapes of thy vineyard, thou shalt not glean it afterward: it shall be for the stranger, for the fatherless, and for the widow." (Deuteronomy 24:19-21) God takes the most care over these people because the world values them the least. "Thou shalt not pervert the judgment of the stranger, nor of the fatherless; nor take a widow's raiment to pledge" (Deuteronomy 24:17) It is written, "Pure religion and undefiled before God and the Father is this, To visit the fatherless and widows in their affliction, and to keep himself unspotted from the world." (James 1:27) The true service of God exists in charity towards our neighbors, especially those who need the help of others (fatherless and widows), and purity of life.

## Lust –

"Thou shalt not covet thy neighbour's house, thou shalt not covet thy neighbour's wife, nor his manservant, nor his maidservant, nor his ox, nor his ass, nor any thing that is thy neighbour's." (Exodus 20:17) This is one of the ten commandments given to us directly from God. This could have been considered under the heading of 'disobedience'. I want to discuss it on its own because of the many scriptural references that included it. We are natural people and as such are subject to certain natural desires. Some of these are the desire for food, water, and companionship. When we lack anything we deem as desirable and necessary, and do not have the means to possess it, lust can be created in our lives. Lust is defined by Unger's Bible Dictionary: "sinful desire – sinful either in being directed toward forbidden objects or in being so violent as to overcome self-control and to engross the mind with earthly, carnal, and perishable things." Another term for 'lust' is 'to covet' (Exodus 20:17; Deuteronomy 5:12). It is not the natural appetites of the body, but the sinful godless inclinations, whether they are of a sensual or spiritual nature, that are considered 'lusts' (Romans 1:24,25). There are no definite objects of lust, but it is the longing for something or someone that is unattainable that is forbidden (Romans 7:7,8). "What shall we say then? is the law sin? God forbid. Nay, I had not known sin, but by the law: for I had not known lust, except the law had said, Thou shalt not covet." (Romans 7:7) Every lust is a product of sin which compels us to obey the desires of the body, "Let not sin therefore reign in your mortal body, that ye should obey it in the lusts thereof." (Romans 6:12) For example: your neighbor has a new car and you like it, this does not constitute a sin. You can have the same car if you have the means to acquire it. However, if you desire his car so much that you steal it, you have committed two sins. You have coveted and you have stolen. Every natural appetite may be perverted by sin into lust, "But put ye on the Lord Jesus Christ, and make not provision for the flesh, to fulfil the lusts thereof." (Romans 13:14) The Israelites had eaten nothing but manna for many years and many miles. They began to miss the bounty of Egypt and lusted after meat being bored of that bread like substance. They were not satisfied with God's provisions (Numbers 10:31-34). Your very soul is in danger if you give into lust. Lust will bring leanness into your soul (Psalm 106:13-15). It is contrary to God's Spirit and will. "For the flesh lusteth against the Spirit, and the Spirit against the flesh: and these are contrary the one to the other: so that ye cannot do the things that ye would." (Galatians 5:17) We cannot allow ourselves to be tempted by our own desires! We will be drawn away from God. "But every man is tempted, when he is drawn away of his own lust, and enticed. Then when lust hath conceived, it bringeth forth sin: and sin, when it is finished, bringeth forth death." (James 1:14,15) It is easy to understand why God would become angry at lust in people! We also, should be so aware of our lustful tendencies and fearful of falling into this trap, that we avoid lust like the plague!! Desire is one thing, lust is quite another! God help us all!!

## Breaking of oaths given in God's name –

One of God's greatest gifts He gives us is the use of His name. We are allowed this honor because we are His children by faith. Just like earthly fathers, the privilege of using the family's credit card comes with responsibility. When you promise something or make a bargain in God's name, you must keep to the contract even if the other party proves to be unfaithful. The people of Gibeon heard that Joshua was on his way to their city. They had heard that he had conquered stronger cities than theirs. They disguised themselves then met with the leaders of Israel to make a peace treaty with them. Then it was discovered that they lied and dealt falsely. The Israelites wanted to kill them. But, the leaders had "sworn to them by the LORD God of Israel..." (Joshua 9:19). The agreement carried a great danger in breaking the promise they had made. "This we will do to them; we will even let them live, lest wrath be upon us, because of the oath which we sware unto them." (Joshua 9:20) A promise made in God's name, then not honored makes God a liar. God forbid! "He is the Rock, his work is perfect: for all his ways are judgment: a GOD of truth and without iniquity, just and right is he." (Deuteronomy 32:4) By making the pledge in His name, God becomes responsible for fulfilling the promise. God will hold you responsible for its conditions and fulfillment, you made the deal. Be careful how you use the name of God.

## Everyone who supports the wicked and hates the Lord –

"And Jehu the son of Hanani the seer went out to meet him, and said to king Jehoshaphat, Shouldest thou help the ungodly, and love them that hate the LORD? therefore is wrath upon thee from before the LORD." (2 Chronicles 19:2) Jehoshaphat was king over Judah. Ahab was king over Israel about the same time. Jehoshaphat followed the ways of the LORD. Not fully, however. He did not destroy the 'high places.' "And he walked in all the ways of Asa his father; he turned not aside from it, doing that which was right in the eyes of the LORD: nevertheless the high places were not taken away; for the people offered and burnt incense yet in the high places." (1 Kings 22:43) Ahab, on the other hand totally disregarded God. He served Baal. "And he did evil in the sight of the LORD, and walked in the way of his father, and in the way of his mother, and in the way of Jeroboam the son of Nebat, who made Israel to sin: for he served Baal, and worshiped him, and provoked to anger the LORD God of Israel, according to all that his father had done." (1 Kings 22:52,53) There came a time when these two kings joined forces to attack Ramoth-gilead. The allegiance of the God fearing with the ungodly will make God angry every time. "Be ye not unequally yoked together with unbelievers: for what fellowship hath righteousness with unrighteousness? and what communion hath light with darkness?" (2 Corinthians 6:14) Therefore, God sent Jehu the son of Hanani to meet Jehoshaphat to condemn him. I want to point out here, that Ahab was killed in the battle but Jehoshaphat survived. God will always look after the righteous. Jehoshaphat reinstituted the Mosaic law and the Levitical priesthood. He went through the country and turned the people back to God. In doing so, he commanded the Levites and judges to be fair and remember that they are God's representatives. "And he charged them, saying, Thus shall ye do in the fear of the LORD, faithfully, and with a perfect heart. And what cause soever shall come to you of your brethren that dwell in their cities, between blood and blood, between law and commandment, statutes and judgments, ye shall even warn them that they trespass not against the LORD, and so wrath come upon you, and upon your brethren: this do, and ye shall not trespass." (2 Chronicles 19:9,10)

## Brothers taking advantage of each other -

Judah had been turned away from God by their king Ahaz. He worshiped other gods and sacrificed to idols. As the Bible puts it "he did not that which was right in the sight of the LORD..." (2 Chronicles 28:1) God punished Judah by allowing Syria and Israel to form an alliance, to defeat Ahaz and take Judah captive to Damascus. Israel also, took captives. This was a sin because Judah and Israel were brothers through Abraham. Israel should have packed up after the battle was won and headed home. But, they did what every other conqueror did! They took the valuables and goods of the city, then took prisoners back to their homeland to be slaves. Naturally this incurred the wrath of God! "And now ye purpose to keep under the children of Judah and Jerusalem for bondmen and bondwomen unto you: but are there not with you, even with you, sins against the LORD your God? Now hear me therefore, and deliver the captives again, which ye have taken captive of your brethren: for the fierce wrath of the LORD is upon you." (2 Chronicles 28:10,11) The prophet Oded, stopped them and admonished the warriors for their sins, the leaders came out against them also. They refused to let the men bring their prisoners, their brothers, into the city. The leaders gave the captives the spoils that Israel had taken, clothed them, fed them and aided them on their journey back to their home. This is a beautiful example of how we should treat our neighbors, Christian or not. Let's first talk about our fellow Christians. We all are tripped and deceived by Satan. That is, after all, his job. When one of our brothers or sisters falls to the temptation, we should treat them as wounded and defeated solders. Again, that is just what they are! We are all soldiers of the cross. If this is not true, then why does Paul tell us to "put on the whole armor of God..." (Ephesians 6:11) It is the policy of The United States Marine Corps that no man gets left behind. Wounded or dead, every man sent on the mission returns to base. This is the policy of the Christian soldier, too? "Brethren, if a man be overtaken in a fault, ye which are spiritual, restore such an one in the spirit of meekness; considering thyself, lest thou also be tempted. Bear ye one another's burdens, and so fulfil the law of Christ." (Galatians 6:1,2) What is the "the law of Christ?" Jesus, Himself, stated it best, "...Thou shalt love thy neighbour as thyself...." (Mark 12:31) Instead of writing the fallen or backslidden off as a casualty of war, we need to love that person and care for their weaknesses and bind their wounds. Never give up on one another. Would you give up on yourself? Again He said, "This is my commandment, That ye love one another, as I have loved you. Greater love hath no man than this, that a man lay down his life for his friends." (John 15:12,13) Concerning, non-Christians, Paul gives us many good pieces of advice. "Bless them which persecute you: bless, and curse not. Rejoice with them that do rejoice, and weep with them that weep. Be of the same mind one toward another. Mind not high things, but condescend to men of low estate. Be not wise in your own conceits. Recompense to no man evil for evil. Provide things honest in the sight of all men. If it be possible, as much as lieth in you, live peaceably with all men. Dearly beloved, avenge not yourselves, but rather give place unto wrath: for it is written, Vengeance is mine; I will repay, saith the LORD. Therefore if thine enemy hunger, feed him; if he thirst, give him drink: for in so doing thou shalt heap coals of fire on his head. Be not overcome of evil, but overcome evil with good." (Romans 12:14-21) The lesson here is to love all mankind. Supporting your fellow Christian, strengthening them with love and testimony. Showing the love of God to those who do not know Him and do not realize that all they do for 'pleasure' or entrainment is an attempt to fill that empty place in them that only God and a personal relationship with Him can fill.

God will supply all our need in this age just as He did in the days of old with Israel. "But my God shall supply all your need according to his riches in glory by Christ Jesus." (Philippians 4:19) We must, however, trust Him fully and walk daily with Him. God is very displeased with those that start to follow Him and then stop. There is a difference in turning away from God and forsaking Him. Turning away implies that we still believe in Him, but we choose to live according to our own thoughts and devices. In forsaking Him, we have decided that there is no God. "God is dead!" was the call of the atheist in the 60's and 70's. The downfall of mankind and great civilizations can all be traced back to the second when they decided that there was no God. No Creator. No higher power that those who were in control, who made laws and ruled over others. God destroyed one such generation with a great flood. It wasn't long after that, those who God chose to save to repopulate the land decided that they were a power unto themselves. Thus we get the story of the Tower of Babel. "And they said, Go to, let us build us a city and a tower, whose top may reach unto heaven; and let us make us a name, lest we be scattered abroad upon the face of the whole earth." (Genesis 11:4) I find it amazing how quickly people forgot the God that saved them. Those who wanted to make a name for themselves were just off the boat, so to speak. Their feet were still wet! Always remember that you are not on this earth at your own whim. You cannot create a tree, bush or blade of grass. The very breath you breath comes from some source outside of yourself. Always seek that higher power. "...The hand of our God is upon all them for good that seek him; but his power and his wrath is against all them that forsake him." (Ezra 8:22) Ezekiel warned, "In thee have they taken gifts to shed blood; thou hast taken usury and increase, and thou hast greedily gained of thy neighbors by extortion, and hast forgotten me, saith the LORD God. Behold, therefore I have smitten mine hand at thy dishonest gain which thou hast made, and at thy blood which hath been in the midst of thee. Can thine heart endure, or can thine hands be strong, in the days that I shall deal with thee? I the LORD have spoken it, and will do it." (Ezekiel 22:12-14) Fear Him, respect Him, and never forsake Him!

## Respect of person –

God's wrath was kindled against the friends of Job because they looked and judged Job's afflictions from his outward appearance rather than his inward righteousness. This essentially constituted respect of persons. God does not judge men by their appearance. He judges them by their heart. All through the discourse of Job and his friends, he keeps claiming that whatever befalls him, God's love is true and faithful. His friends, however, continually blame Job's afflictions on his own sins or downfalls. God renders judgment and declares that Job "spoken of him the thing that was right" (Job 42:7). He had given a much better and truer account of the divine providence than they had done. They had wronged God by making prosperity a mark of true righteousness and affliction a certain indication of God's wrath; but Job had testified of God correctly by maintaining that God's love and hatred are to be judged by what is in men, not by what is worn of possessed by them. "For all this I considered in my heart even to declare all this, that the righteous, and the wise, and their works, are in the hand of God: no man knoweth either love or hatred by all that is before them. All things come alike to all: there is one event to the righteous, and to the wicked; to the good and to the clean, and to the unclean; to him that sacrificeth, and to him that sacrificeth not: as is the good, so is the sinner; and he that sweareth, as he that feareth an oath. This is an evil among all things that are done under the sun, that there is one event unto all: yea, also the heart of the sons of men is full of evil, and madness is in their heart while they live, and after that they go to the dead." (Ecclesiastes 9:1-3) The largest church is not the best, the smallest is not the worst. The man in the limousine is no more righteous than the man walking from place to place. Jesus said, "Judge not, that ye be not judged." (Matthew 7:1) Again, Ecclesiastes 9:2 tells us, "All things come alike to all: there is one event to the righteous, and to the wicked..." Looking only on the outward appearance of a person and coming to a conclusion about his or her spiritual condition will give an incomplete picture of that person. Only God can look inside and know a person's heart. Again Jesus advises us to, "Judge not according to the appearance, but judge righteous judgment." (John 7:24) We do not know a person's whole story, nor can we ever. Actually it is none of our business. When we judge a stranger, sinner or believer, we are stepping into God's shoes and no one can fill those. Only God judges! Only God can say who is righteous or who is wicked! God and God alone will decide who will be saved and who will be lost. All we can do is love all mankind and live our lives as an example to others.

## Dealing unfairly with your neighbor –

Boundaries were set when the land was divided among the tribes of Israel as they came out of Egypt. These were assigned by God. "Thou shalt not remove thy neighbour's landmark, which they of old time have set in thine inheritance, which thou shalt inherit in the land that the LORD thy God giveth thee to possess it." (Deuteronomy 19:14) King Jeroboam continued the traditions and idolatry of past kings. He even mixed idolatry into the religious practices of the temple. He brought back the golden calves and discouraged the pilgrimage of the people to the temple at Jerusalem by putting shrines in Dan and Bethel. These cities were at the extremes of the country. "The princes of Judah were like them that remove the bound: therefore I will pour out my wrath upon them like water." (Hosea 5:10) This was moving the boundaries of God. Men still try this today. God will forgive me if I do this or that, it's not mentioned specifically in the Bible, they will say. Or, all I have to do is pray for forgiveness. He will forgive the sins of His people, but once forgiven the act cannot be willfully repeated with the expectation of forgiveness. People today, as they did way back then, pick and choose the commandments they want to obey and ignore the ones they don't like.

## Men who hold the truth in unrighteousness –

There have always been people who deny the existence and power of God. "Men who hold the truth in unrighteousness", as Paul calls them in Romans 1:18. Those who would pervert the gospel and rewrite the laws that God has previously set forth as the way to follow Him and thus attain entrance into His presence in heaven. Creation itself proves the existence of a living God. In the spring we can see His work in the awaking flowers and trees. In the winter we can see His work by the dormancy of the plant life and the hibernation of the animals. All things are done in a manner to protect during the winter so as to produce life again in the spring. Believers know this is the work of God, the unbeliever calls this 'mother nature'. The truth of God is denied at every turn by the 'experts'. Paul says that of these that they professed themselves to be wise, but actually they became fools. (Romans 1:21,22) The 'men of science' have been trying to figure out God's secrets of creation for a long, long time and have yet to find out His ways. If our 'wise' men cannot figure out Genesis 1:1, how can they get the rest of God's works right!? Because all of creation testifies of God and there are those who do not believe, God's wrath is against them, "For the wrath of God is revealed from heaven against all ungodliness and unrighteousness of men, who hold the truth in unrighteousness; Because that which may be known of God is manifest in them; for God hath showed it unto them." (Romans 1:18,19) Our Creator has shown Himself in many ways since the beginning of time. There are many people who do not believe that God exists, yet you will hear them use scripture in their conversation. We recently had a political candidate put forth a whole platform on 'hope, faith and charity'. Where have we read these words before? Because man has made the glory of the incorruptible God into the image of corruptible things, "God gave them up to uncleanness through the lusts of their own hearts" (Romans 1:23,24). It is easy to fall into the 'science knows best' trap. Everyone around you is talking about 'the big bang theory', 'global warming' and other scientific theories. Keep in mind the definition of the word 'theory' is a speculative idea or plan as to how something might be done; mere conjecture or a guess (according to Webster's New World Dictionary). These great men of science are not sure, they are speculating. In other words, they are just guessing, using the extent of their limited knowledge. Do we have to guess that God is real and at work in this earth? Do we really believe that God is too weak to protect that which He has created? Our God is all knowing and all powerful! The truth is all around us. We cannot deny His existence or His work. Thank God for His patience and His mercies!! "For I am not ashamed of the gospel of Christ: for it is the power of God unto salvation to everyone that believeth; to the Jew first, and also to the Greek. For therein is the righteousness of God revealed from faith to faith: as it is written, The just shall live by faith." (Romans 1:16,17)

## Those who disobey the truth –

The truth of God surrounds us, as was the theme of the preceding discussion. There are those people who still choose to live according to their own understanding. Who want to live by their own laws or pick and choose the laws of God which they will honor and obey. We all know people who tell us that the

Old Testament was for the olden days and the New Testament is for today. A careful study of the teachings of Jesus will reveal that His references came straight from the Old Testament. Therefore, those who make such comments are denying and disobeying the truth. I'm sure that there are many more examples that can be offered. God's wrath is toward anybody that does such things (Romans 2:8). Paul wrote that the riches of His goodness and forbearance and longsuffering leads to repentance (Romans 2:4). It is the hardness and impenitent heart of the unrighteous that lays up wrath against him to the day of judgment, "the righteous judgment of God" (Romans 2:5). We are given a warning by Paul of the rewards and punishments of men when we stand before God to be judged. He writes, "Who will render to every man according to his deeds: to them who by patient continuance in well doing seek for glory and honor and immortality, eternal life: but unto them that are contentious, and do not obey the truth, but obey unrighteousness, indignation and wrath, tribulation and anguish, upon every soul of man that doeth evil, of the Jew first, and also of the Gentile; but glory, honor, and peace, to every man that worketh good, to the Jew first, and also to the Gentile: for there is no respect of persons with God." (Romans 2:6-11) Which group do you want to be in? Those who patiently continue to do well or those that are contentious, and do not obey the truth? The choice is truly yours, but the consequences have been established for thousands of years.

## Those who persecute God's people –

When you give your life to Jesus, the people whom you associated with before will not understand the change they see in you. They will call you foolish or deranged. You might even be called a heretic. That's all right. In Revelation 18:4 we are told to "come out of her, my people..." Unless the people you were associated with before were spiritual people, it will appear to them as if you are trying to be 'holier than thou.' Actually your conversion convicts and condemns them. They can have the same thing, be the same way, live the same life. They can give their lives to Christ, also. God has no respect of persons. He would have all men saved. It is easier, however, to accuse and persecute believers than to surrender to Christ Jesus and be saved. Paul, the great apostle of God to the Gentiles started out as a zealot for the Jewish way. He was at the stoning of Stephen. He held the coats of those who actually did the deed. He ask the priests for a letter of authority to hunt, chase and kill believers of Jesus. That was why he was on the road to Damascus when Jesus confronted and converted him. There are still places where you will be persecuted or killed for being a Christian in this world. Try building a Christian church in a Muslim country! This way of life is not for the weak or faint of heart. But, fear not, God will repay those who hurt His people. "For ye, brethren, became followers of the churches of God which in Judea are in Christ Jesus: for ye also have suffered like things of your own countrymen, even as they have of the Jews: who both killed the LORD Jesus, and their own prophets, and have persecuted us; and they please not God, and are contrary to all men: forbidding us to speak to the Gentiles that they might be saved, to fill up their sins alway: for the wrath is come upon them to the uttermost." (1 Thessalonians 2:14-16) Vengeance is the LORD's responsibility. "Dearly beloved, avenge not yourselves, but rather give place unto wrath: for it is written, Vengeance is mine; I will repay, saith the LORD." (Romans 12:19) Give your life to Christ and let Him handle the details.

## Those who take the mark of the beast and their leaders –

The last days will be marked by evil controlling the earth, the spirit of the anti-Christ ruling and Christians being killed and persecuted. No commerce will take place unless you have the mark of the beast either in your right hand or in your forehead. The use of the word 'in' is not a mistranslation or lack of understanding. For a long time it was considered that the mark would be a tattoo or a permanent stamp of some kind. Technology has caught up to God. There are devices today which are injected under your skin and contain all your personal health information. They are referred to as RFID chips (Radio Frequency Identification). You probably have already come in contact with the retailer's version if you have bought a television, computer, some drugs, CD or video game. Remember when the clerk ran the box over the deactivation device so you could leave the store without setting off the alarm? How much of a stretch will it be to combine the medical version with the retail version and add your bank information? We can pay our bills online now! I ask you, is this the beginning of the mark of the beast? How about this announcement from Intermec; "Intermec Releases Software That Targets Tags of Interest The ARX reader system includes motion detection that pinpoints tags based on their movement. The company also plans to release a new higher-memory tag and a lower-cost reader." Twice in Revelation are warned to be patient and maintain faith. "...Here is the patience and the faith of the saints" (Revelation 13:10) "Here is the patience of the saints: here are they that keep the commandments of God, and the faith of Jesus." (Revelation 14:12) Those who take the mark may be able to buy sell and live a comfortable life on this earth, but they will be lost when Jesus returns. We Christians have to come up with a way to get what we will need without taking the mark. Maybe a barter system and keeping a very low profile. We could just make up our minds as that day comes that we are going to die and wait for Jesus. "And the third angel followed them, saying with a loud voice, If any man worship the beast and his image, and receive his mark in his forehead, or in his hand, the same shall drink of the wine of the wrath of God, which is poured out without mixture into the cup of his indignation; and he shall be tormented with fire and brimstone in the presence of the holy angels, and in the presence of the Lamb: and the smoke of their torment ascendeth up for ever and ever: and they have no rest day nor night, who worship the beast and his image, and whosoever receiveth the mark of his name." (Revelation 14:9-11)

## Those who would destroy God's people -

The king of Assyria thought to destroy the people of Jerusalem and control the city. In his mind this should be an easy task. He had waged war against more powerful kingdoms and defeated them. Hezekiah (the king of Judah) heard that the cities and kingdoms around him were being defeated by Sennacherib (the King of Assyria), he sent a message begging him for a treaty. Sennacherib demanded so much gold and silver in payment that Hezekiah sent the whole treasury and looted the temple of God, even to the stripping of gold off the door and pillars. Hezekiah thought he was safe, after all he had paid off his enemy. Sennacherib sent three officers and 'a great host against Jerusalem' (2 Kings 18:17). The money was not enough. Sennacherib wanted the city! Hezekiah had nothing more to bargain with, the gold and silver was gone. The message from Sennacherib demanded the people to surrender, and said that depending upon God would be futile and trust in Hezekiah would lead them to destruction because he had torn down the 'high places' of God. He didn't realize that the 'high places' were for the worship of idols. Hezekiah had turned Judah back to the true living God. Only now does it occur to Hezekiah to go to God! He tried to buy his way out of trouble, that didn't work. With nowhere else to go, he goes where he should have gone in the beginning. He sent his own representatives to Isaiah (the prophet) to inquire of God for him. "And Isaiah said unto them, thus shall ye say to your master, thus saith the LORD, be not afraid of the words which thou hast heard, with which the servants of the king of Assyria have blasphemed me. Behold, I will send a blast upon him, and he shall hear a rumor, and shall return to his own land; and I will cause him to fall by the sword in his own land." (2 Kings 19:6,7) When Sennacherib saw no response from Hezekiah, he sent a message to him. "Thus shall ye speak to Hezekiah king of Judah, saying, Let not thy God in whom thou trustest deceive thee, saying, Jerusalem shall not be delivered into the hand of the king of Assyria. Behold, thou hast heard what the kings of Assyria have done to all lands, by destroying them utterly: and shalt thou be delivered? Have the gods of the nations delivered them which my fathers have destroyed; as Gozan, and Haran, and Rezeph, and the children of Eden which were in Thelasar? Where is the king of Hamath, and the king of Arpad, and the king of the city of Sepharvaim, of Hena, and Ivah?" (2 Kings 19:10-13) God had Hezekiah and Judah protected all the while because Hezekiah had done right in the sight of the LORD. But, Hezekiah, being human and afraid of the approaching armies, went into the temple, himself, to inquire of the LORD. I like what he did with the letter he received. "And Hezekiah received the letter of the hand of the messengers, and read it: and Hezekiah went up into the house of the LORD, and spread it before the LORD. And Hezekiah prayed before the LORD..." (2 Kings 19:14,15) This is a good example of what we should do when we have a problem or are faced with a seemingly insurmountable situation. Give it to God!! Hezekiah was praying in an empty temple, he could not perform a sacrifice if he wanted to. He had sent all the valuables to Sennacherib. You would think that God would let him be defeated because he had stolen from God when he looted the temple. God was faithful to him and sent him an answer. "Then Isaiah the son of Amoz sent to Hezekiah, saying, Thus saith the LORD God of Israel, That which thou hast prayed to me against Sennacherib king of Assyria I have heard." (2 Kings 19:20) The looting of the temple was totally unnecessary. Sennacherib never came close to Judah. God took control and kept him away from the city. "And it came to pass that night, that the angel of the LORD went out, and smote in the camp of the Assyrians an hundred fourscore and six thousand: and when they arose early in the morning, behold, they were all dead corpses. So Sennacherib king of Assyria departed, and went and returned, and dwelt at Nineveh." (2 Kings 19:35,36) Hezekiah disappointed God because he had a temporary lack of faith and tried to handle the situation on his own. But, it was Sennacherib that really made God mad. First he had purposed in his heart to destroy God's chosen people and chosen city, then he blasphemed God. God said of Sennacherib, "But I know thy abode, and thy going out, and thy coming in, and thy rage against me. Because thy rage against me and thy tumult is come up into mine ears, therefore I will put my hook in thy nose, and my bridle in thy lips, and I will turn thee back by the way by which thou camest." (2 Kings 19:27,28)

## The rage of the tongue -

The tongue is a thing to be feared, spiritually speaking. With it we can bless, strengthen and give comfort to others. We can teach, correct and encourage one another. With the same body part we can curse, deride and destroy. While the tongue is a small part of the body, it is accompanied by a great responsibility. "For in many things we offend all. If any man offend not in word, the same is a perfect man, and able also to bridle the whole body. Behold, we put bits in the horses' mouths, that they may obey us; and we turn about their whole body. Behold also the ships, which though they be so great, and are driven of fierce winds, yet are they turned about with a very small helm, whithersoever the governor listeth. Even so the tongue is a little member, and boasteth great things. Behold, how great a matter a little fire kindleth! And the tongue is a fire, a world of iniquity: so is the tongue among our members, that it defileth the whole body, and setteth on fire the course of nature; and it is set on fire of hell. For every kind of beasts, and of birds, and of serpents, and of things in the sea, is tamed, and hath been tamed of mankind: but the tongue can no man tame; it is an unruly evil, full of deadly poison. Therewith bless we God, even the Father; and therewith curse we men, which are made after the similitude of God. Out of the same mouth proceedeth blessing and cursing. My brethren, these things ought not so to be." (James 3:2-10) When God punished Israel by sending them into a foreign land, the leaders cursed God. They cried out to Him, not for deliverance, but to blame Him for their present situation. "They return, but not to the most High: they are like a deceitful bow: their princes shall fall by the sword for the rage of their tongue: this shall be their derision in the land of Egypt." (Hosea 7:16) When hard times come upon us, it's easy to blame God. Why is it we do not look inside ourselves for the reason that we are not being blessed by God or why He withdrew His protection? "These six things doth the LORD hate: yea, seven are an abomination unto him: A proud look, a lying tongue, and hands that shed innocent blood, an heart that deviseth wicked imaginations, feet that be swift in running to mischief, a false witness that speaketh lies, and he that soweth discord among brethren." (Proverbs 6:16-19) We must be extremely careful what we say and how we say it! "Finally, be ye all of one mind, having compassion one of another, love as brethren, be pitiful, be courteous: not rendering evil for evil, or railing for railing: but contrariwise blessing; knowing that ye are thereunto called, that ye should inherit a blessing. For he that will love life, and see good days, let him refrain his tongue from evil, and his lips that they speak no guile: let him eschew evil, and do good; let him seek peace, and ensue it. For the eyes of the LORD are over the righteous, and his ears are open unto their prayers: but the face of the LORD is against them that do evil." (1 Peter 3:8-12) Peter pretty well summed it up. I cannot add anything!

I just pray that God will teach us all to control our tongues and speak as He would have us to.

## Complaining and dissatisfaction with God's provisions –

The children of Israel wandered in the wilderness forty years. They were tired, bored and disgusted with walking, walking and never getting to the land promised them many, many years before. They were promised a land flowing with milk and honey. All they had seen for forty years was sand, sand and more sand. God had supplied manna for food. Forty years of the same food got pretty boring and took its toll. Their stomachs caused them to look back and remember what they had eaten in Egypt. "We remember the fish, which we did eat in Egypt freely; the cucumbers, and the melons, and the leeks, and the onions, and the garlic: But now our soul is dried away: there is nothing at all, beside this manna, before our eyes." (Numbers 11:5,6) They had forgotten that they were slaves and badly treated there. They were listening to their appetites instead of God. The stomach can be a powerful motivator! The desire of their hearts went back to captivity instead of remembering that God had saved them from torture and degradation. They complained about God's provisions and lusted for meat (Numbers 11:4). God heard their complaint and supplied them with quails (Numbers 11:31,32). This came at a very high price! "And while the flesh was yet between their teeth, ere it was chewed, the wrath of the LORD was kindled against the people, and the LORD smote the people with a very great plague." (Numbers 11:33) God was angered by their complaining and sent fire to destroy the complainers (Numbers 11:1). Our LORD does not take complaining lightly. In this example He sent fire to destroy the complainers and then sent a plague to destroy those who lusted after flesh. Paul admonishes us to, "Do all things without murmurings and disputings ..." (Philippians 2:14)

## Adultery covered up by murder –

David was the king of Israel. He had many wives and concubines, there was no reason that he should lack for company or female companionship. One evening he was on his roof enjoying the weather. He looked to the roof of a neighboring house and saw a woman bathing (2 Samuel 11:2). With all the women at his beck and call, he desired the one he had just seen. David inquired after her and was told that she was married (2 Samuel 11:3). That did not stop him from having to have her (2 Samuel 11:4). David knew the commandment, "Thou shalt not commit adultery." (Exodus 20:14), this did not stop him, either. He had her brought to him and committed the deed. Guilt overcame him and he tried to cover his sin by being generous to her husband, Uriah. He gave him leave to go home and be with his wife, Bath-Sheba (2 Samuel 11:6,8). Uriah was a good soldier and would not leave his post or his king while the country was at war (2 Samuel 11:9-11). David had gotten Bath-Sheba pregnant and thought to cover his sin by having Uriah have relations with Bath-Sheba and thereby make it look as though the baby was Uriah's. When that plan did not work, he sent Uriah back into battle with instructions for his commander to assign him to a position where he would surely be killed (2 Samuel 11:14-17). With Uriah dead, Bath-Sheba would be free to be with David. This did not set well with God! God sent a prophet to David to convict him of his sin (2 Samuel 12:1-9). David repented (2 Samuel 12:13). God demanded retribution and took the son that was conceived in sin (2 Samuel 12:14,15,18,19). David broke many of the commandments with this sin. First, he coveted his neighbor's wife; second, he committed adultery; thirdly, he committed murder. "Thou shalt not covet thy neighbour's house, thou shalt not covet thy neighbour's wife, nor his manservant, nor his maidservant, nor his ox, nor his ass, nor any thing that is thy neighbour's." (Exodus 20:17) "Thou shalt not commit adultery."

(Exodus 20:14) "Thou shalt not kill." (Exodus 20:13) This does not take into account that he idolized human flesh and took his eyes off God. We know our God as a loving God. How mad was God at David and Bath-Sheba that He would take an innocent life!!

## No Judgment –

"Behold, the LORD'S hand is not shortened, that it cannot save; neither his ear heavy, that it cannot hear: but your iniquities have separated between you and your God, and your sins have hid his face from you, that he will not hear." (Isaiah 59:1,2) God does not separate Himself from us, we push Him away. He wants to spend time with us and bless us. When we sin, He has to leave! He is without sin and therefore cannot stay where sin is. Even though we are followers of Christ, we still have free choice. We are not robots. Thank God we have a way to get back into God's good graces when we slip and sin. However we must be aware of our iniquities and utilize the path back to Him. When we lack judgment and fail to return to Him, He is greatly displeased (Isaiah 59:15). Our sins are increased (multiplied) before Him (Isaiah 59:12). We are not innocent, we know exactly what we have done against God. The basic sins are always the same. First we get too busy to read His word or pray, then we are too tired to attend church. Eventually, we just don't care about anything spiritual or Godly. "For our transgressions are multiplied before thee, and our sins testify against us: for our transgressions are with us; and as for our iniquities, we know them; in transgressing and lying against the LORD, and departing away from our God, speaking oppression and revolt, conceiving and uttering from the heart words of falsehood." (Isaiah 59:12,13) When we do commit an offense against God, we try to justify it. 'An innocent lie or white lie.' This is what the verse refers to as "...transgressing and lying against the LORD..." How about staying out of Church or not praying or reading God's Word, could these not be considered "departing away from our God?" Are you dissatisfied with your Pastor when he speaks the Biblical truth and it hurts your feelings? Do you talk against him and about leaving his congregation? Could this not be considered " speaking oppression and revolt?" Have you ever exaggerated to make yourself look good or to put someone down? Does this verse not say that one of the sins are "conceiving and uttering from the heart words of falsehood?" When men do wickedly and do not consider God, ask for justice or beg for truth, judgment will not be found. "None calleth for justice, nor any pleadeth for truth: they trust in vanity, and speak lies; they conceive mischief, and bring forth iniquity." (Isaiah 59:4) To follow up, "And judgment is turned away backward, and justice standeth afar off: for truth is fallen in the street, and equity cannot enter. Yea, truth faileth; and he that departeth from evil maketh himself a prey: and the LORD saw it, and it displeased him that there was no judgment." (Isaiah 59:14,15) Where no judgment exists there is no right or wrong, no truths. It's all good!! Sound familiar?

## The heathen that is at ease -

The Israelites were taken captive at various times in their history. When they had sinned against God, He punished them by letting them be defeated and carried away captive by some neighboring country. The sin was usually idolatry or turning away from God and His commandments. When God lead the Israelites into the promised land, He had commanded them to worship and serve Him. If they did that they would live safe in their homeland. If they did not, they would be taken away from their comfort and into captivity. His purpose was to make them uncomfortable in their strange surroundings so they would turn back to Him and call on Him for salvation. Israel was in captivity in Persia (Iran) for seventy years (Zechariah 1:12). They had become comfortable in their captivity. Therefore, they did not miss their homeland or God. Had they turned back to Him, God would have caused some affliction to come upon the Persians. This was not the case, "the heathen" was at ease (Zechariah 1:11,15). God promised to deliver Israel (Zechariah 2:6-9). God will send something against us too, if we forget about Him or turn from Him. However, He will deliver us also, if we turn again to Him and call to Him for help and deliverance. We must try not to transgress against God! If we do, however, He is always there ready to forgive us and deliver us again into His grace and presence. Praise the LORD!!

## Covetousness and dealing falsely –

God gave the Israelites specific instructions as how to live and conduct themselves in the land He gave them for their inheritance. We commonly call them the 'ten commandments'. They were promised that if they obeyed them, they would live long on the land and be safe from their enemies. This has been discussed so many times in this chapter that I will not go into it any further. Let me just say that all of Israel had sinned against God and He was about to send them into captivity once again. This time, into Babylon (Iraq). He accused them of covetousness (greedy for gain) and their spiritual leaders of prophesying falsely (for gain) (Jeremiah 6:13). For the right fee they would tell the people what they wanted to hear (Jeremiah 5:30,31). The people did not find this situation disagreeable (Jeremiah 5:31). God, however did and this made Him very angry! Still, He tried to get them to see the error of their ways and return to His ways and righteousness. Of course, their hard hearts refused (Jeremiah 6:10,16,17). Twice He entreated them to return and twice they refused. God had no choice but to punish them! (Jeremiah 6:19) Our God is a merciful God and does not <u>want</u> to punish us when we sin. He has no choice, however! He is sinless and cannot be around sin. He will give us warnings if we listen. He will give us at least two chances to turn from our sins and to Him. If we do not heed His call, our fate is our responsibility. THANK GOD FOR HIS MERCY AND PATIENCE!!

## Iniquity -

God cannot bear iniquity (sin, wickedness). There are various sections above where certain sins are singled out and discussed. Jeremiah 25:12-16 tells the Israelites that God will release them from their captivity. Then punish the nation that held them captive. We all know that God hates sin! It made Him so mad on one occasion He destroyed the earth with a flood (Genesis 6:5-8). Satan brought sin into God's kingdom when he decided he was just as good as God (see the explanation on pride). He carried this condition to earth when he and his followers were cast out of heaven. When sin and wickedness grew again to infect the earth, God sacrificed His Son to defeat Satan and save mankind, "For God so loved the world, that he gave his only begotten Son, that whosoever believeth in him should not perish, but have everlasting life. For God sent not his Son into the world to condemn the world; but that the world through him might be saved." (John 3:16,17) This is just more proof that God gives man every chance to be delivered from the evil that Satan brought to this earth when he fell from heaven.

## Dealing by revenge and with a spiteful heart -

The Philistines' constant harassment of Israel made God angry. The Philistines were a close neighbor to Israel but were not a native of the land, even though they had occupied the land since the time of Abraham (Genesis 10:13,14). They were a powerful sea going people probably from Crete. They settled along the coast between the Mediterranean Sea and Israel. This gave them control over shipping, land trade and major advancements, such as iron smelting (for weapons). Then, as today, differences of opinion over the true God caused disputes and, naturally, wars. The Philistines worshiped various gods. Among them were Dagon (the grain deity), Ashtaroth (the ancient Assyrian goddess of propagation, Ishtar), and Beelzebub (the ruler of demons, we know him today as Satan). There will always be trouble when Satan is in close proximity to God's people!! It is no stretch of the imagination to say that the Philistines hated the Israelites. This was heightened by David's defeat of Goliath. "Thus saith the LORD God; Because the Philistines have dealt by revenge, and have taken vengeance with a despiteful heart, to destroy it for the old hatred; therefore thus saith the LORD God; Behold, I will stretch out mine hand upon the Philistines, and I will cut off the Cherethims, and destroy the remnant of the sea coast. And I will execute great vengeance upon them with furious rebukes; and they shall know that I am the LORD, when I shall lay my vengeance upon them." (Ezekiel 25:15-17)

### Final observations –

We have just discussed many reason's that God became angry. All of them have to do with His people turning away from Him or disobeying Him in one way or another. As laid out in Leviticus 26:3-39, God will bless the obedient and punish the disobedient. The blessings come immediately but the curses (punishments) are administered in six steps. Basically, His blessings are removed from you little by little. "But if ye will not hearken unto me, and will not do all these commandments; And if ye shall despise my statutes, or if your soul abhor my judgments, so that ye will not do all my commandments, but that ye break my covenant: I also will do this unto you..." (Leviticus 26:14-16a)

God is very patient as it is exhibited in these verses. He gives the disobedient, sinful person plenty of opportunities and time to repent. God warns of six punishments to come to those who do not follow Him, and after each punishment He gives the people time to return to Him, thus stopping the remaining punishments. How is that for patience!! The first chastisement God brings is distress to those who disobey, "...I will even appoint over you terror, consumption, and the burning ague, that shall consume the eyes, and cause sorrow of heart: and ye shall sow your seed in vain, for your enemies shall eat it. And I will set my face against you, and ye shall be slain before your enemies: they that hate you shall reign over you; and ye shall flee when none pursueth you." (Leviticus 26:16,17) The word translated as 'consumption' means emaciation, to cause to become abnormally lean usually by starvation or disease. 'Burning ague' means fever. You would think that the warning of these conditions would be enough to keep believers wanting to be obedient. However, there are those who are hardhearted and obstinate.

God gives a them second chance. If the distress they are experiencing is not enough to convince them that they have sinned against God, there will be a drought and the land will be barren. "And if ye will not yet for all this hearken unto me, then I will punish you seven times more for your sins. And I will break the pride of your power; and I will make your heaven as iron, and your earth as brass: And your strength shall be spent in vain: for your land shall not yield her increase, neither shall the trees of the land yield their fruits." (Leviticus 26:18-20) "... the pride of your power..." refers to the item or person that make you feel comfortable and confident in your strength. It could be a storage barn full of grain or a vineyard full of grapes. By today's standards the pride of your power could be a large bank account, home, success in your job or successful children. As a nation, the pride of your power could be a large and powerful standing army. God says He will destroy whatever is making you too proud to worship Him and obey His commandments. Don't you think that losing your health, comfort and safety, your land, and food and water would be enough to make a convert of anyone? Well, if this is not enough to bring them to their senses, God gives them another chance.

For the third chastisement He will send wild beasts to them. "And if ye walk contrary unto me, and will not hearken unto me; I will bring seven times more plagues upon you according to your sins. I will also send wild beasts among you, which shall rob you of your children, and destroy your cattle, and make you few in number; and your high ways shall be desolate." (Leviticus 26:21,22) The beasts will essentially besiege the people so that they will lose their children and other members of their families and their livelihood. The dangerous beasts will scare away travelers, thereby, stopping trade and commerce and making the people poor. Are you convinced that God has a grievance against you, now?! Are you wondering what has happened to you? Are you asking yourself, "What next?" Would you believe that God offers another opportunity to return to Him?!?

A fourth opportunity!? Understanding that their hearts are hardened and they still refuse to acknowledge that they have sinned against God, He sends war and disease among them, "And if ye will not be reformed by me by these things, but will walk contrary unto me; Then will I also walk contrary unto you, and will punish you yet seven times for your sins. And I will bring a sword upon you, that shall avenge the quarrel of my covenant: and when ye are gathered together within your cities, I will send the pestilence among you; and ye shall be delivered into the hand of the enemy. And when I have broken the staff of your bread, ten women shall bake your bread in one oven, and they shall deliver you your bread again by weight: and ye shall eat, and not be satisfied." (Leviticus 26:23-26) Those who are not driven into the cities by the wild beasts will be forced in by invading armies. " I will bring a sword upon you..." Once all are thought to be safe within the wall of the city, God says He will send a pestilence or disease into them. How much clearer can He say it. "...when ye are gathered together within your cities, I will send the pestilence among you..." Your food will be rationed, "...they shall deliver you your bread again by weight..." Do you see how the blessings that come from obedience are being taken away through disobedience? This is God's doing, but not God's fault! Not ready to acknowledge God yet? He gives you another chance! What glorious mercy!!

You have resisted His calls though distress, drought, wild beasts, disease and now He will bring famine to you, "And if ye will not for all this hearken unto me, but walk contrary unto me; Then I will walk contrary unto you also in fury; and I, even I, will chastise you seven times for your sins. And ye shall eat the flesh of your sons, and the flesh of your daughters shall ye eat. And I will destroy your high places, and cut down your images, and cast your carcases upon the carcases of your idols, and my soul shall abhor you. And I will make your cities waste, and bring your sanctuaries unto desolation, and I will not smell the savour of your sweet odours." (Leviticus 26:27-31) He just now starts to turn away from the sinner, "... my soul shall abhor you..." He refuses to honor their sacrifices, "...I will not smell the savour of your sweet odours." The present day follower of Jesus Christ is not required to obey the laws of Moses or perform the sacrifices demanded in ancient days. Jesus is our sacrifice! He paid the cost of sin for all of us for all times. Through his death and resurrection and our faith in Him we have a direct line to the Father. "Christ hath redeemed us from the curse of the law..." (Galatians 3:13) Jesus Christ is our advocate with the Father to intercede for us when we slip into sin. "My little children, these things write I unto you, that ye sin not. And if any man sin, we have an advocate with the Father, Jesus Christ the righteous" (1 John 2:1) God decides that there is nothing that will bring these stiff necked people back to Him. So the final punishment is to be removed from the land that they were promised through Moses and secured by Joshua.

God will send the hardhearted, stiff necked, disobedient sinner away from all his comfort and security and make him a slave to a foreign power, usually one who hates him, "And I will bring the land into desolation: and your enemies which dwell therein shall be astonished at it. And I will scatter you among the heathen, and will draw out a sword after you: and your land shall be desolate, and your cities waste. Then shall the land enjoy her sabbaths, as long as it lieth desolate, and ye be in your enemies' land; even then shall the land rest, and enjoy her sabbaths. As long as it lieth desolate it shall rest; because it did not rest in your sabbaths, when ye dwelt upon it. And upon them that are left alive of you I will send a faintness into their hearts in the lands of their enemies; and the sound of a shaken leaf shall chase them; and they shall flee, as fleeing from a sword; and they shall fall when none pursueth. And they shall fall one upon another, as it were before a sword, when none pursueth: and ye shall have no power to stand before your enemies. And ye shall perish among the heathen, and the land of your enemies shall eat you up. And they that are left of you shall pine away in their iniquity in your enemies' lands; and also in the iniquities of their fathers shall they pine away with them." (Leviticus 26:32-39) He has given the sinner five opportunities to acknowledge that He is God and return to Him before He sends them the last punishment; exile. God never fully turns His back on them. He is always there to restore the repentant when they turn to Him (Leviticus 26:40-45). The punishments experienced by the sinful then are distress, drought, wild beasts, disease, famine, and finally exile.

There are different degrees of God's anger as you can see. They are displeasure, indignation, anger, rage, fury and wrath. They were exhibited throughout this discussion. We can observe how God's anger grew with the sinfulness of His people. From displeasure with the wayward to the wrath of God expelling them from out of the promised land. As the people's sins became more offensive, God's anger became more fierce. Our God is very slow to anger. There are many verses in the Bible that tell us this. I did not realize just how slow until I studied this subject. This is the verse that speaks to the speed of God's anger that is my favorite, "The LORD is gracious, and full of compassion; slow to anger, and of great mercy." (Psalms 145:8) Another verse that I like that describes God's attributes is, "The LORD is slow to anger, and great in power, and will not at all acquit the wicked: the LORD hath his way in the whirlwind and in the storm, and the clouds are the dust of his feet." (Nahum 1:3) The Bible so beautifully explains itself and defines the terms used. The trick is to be closely observant and in tune with the Holy Spirit. Why was wrath the last type of anger that God released on the hardhearted, disobedient people? The answer is found in Nahum, "God is jealous, and the LORD revengeth; the LORD revengeth, and is furious; the LORD will take vengeance on his adversaries, and he reserveth wrath for his enemies." (Nahum 1:2) The people had turned so far away from God that they actually became His enemies. People, as God's creation, should be like God because we are made in His image (Genesis 1:26). If God is slow to anger, then we better be also. There are, also, verses that speak to man's speed of anger. They are found in Proverbs. My favorite one is, "He that is slow to anger is better than the mighty; and he that ruleth his spirit than he that taketh a city." (Proverbs 16:32) I prefer this one because it refers to the self-control that is required to hold one's peace. It is easy to blow off steam and let the chips fall where they may. It takes a lot of internal fortitude to keep quiet when what you really want to do is to read someone the riot act. Again it is stated, "A wrathful man stirreth up strife: but he that is slow to anger appeaseth strife." (Proverbs 15:18) As I stated earlier that, reading and studying all these verses about anger did not increase my anger. Actually, they had a calming effect upon my spirit. I still get displeased with situations from time to time, but I do not blow up into that extreme rage. A serious desire to serve God and a concentrated effort to understand the will of God for my anger management along with all the many, many anger verses overwhelmed the evil left within me that I had not fully crucified when I accepted Christ as my personal Savior. "And they that are Christ's have crucified the flesh with the affections and lusts." (Galatians 5:24)

I pray that you will receive the same results as you continue reading this book. If your anger is severe, that God will give you peace and self-control. If your anger is just mild, that God will increase your patience and love. In all things may God give you understanding and wisdom. We now know what makes God angry. Let's examine what made the characters in the Bible stories angry.

# WHAT MADE THE
# BIBLE CHARACTERS ANGRY

These were average everyday people just like you and me. Granted, some were kings and others were in positions of power. However, their emotions, drives and desires are just like ours. With this in mind, we can say that the things that angered them, are active in our lives. We are them... they are us!!

There are more than one person involved in some reasons, I have chosen to deal with each person's story and situation separately. In the last chapter, the only person to get angry was God. This chapter will deal with many, as you will see. May God bless you and help you to hold your peace. Amen.

## Injustice -

**Jacob stole Esau's blessing –** No one will deny that when an injustice is done, the injured party has a right to be angry. How mad do you think you would be if you would be harmed twice by the same person? I'm referring to the story of Esau and Jacob. Esau was a hunter, a man of the land and Jacob was a quiet man preferring the domestic life and duties (Genesis 25:27). Hunting is a hit or miss endeavor. Some days you might find your game quickly and others you might not see any at all.

Domestic life is more sure. You can depend on meals and steady work tending the homestead. There came a day when Esau had one of those bad hunting days and came home empty. This, of course, meant he had not eaten all day. Jacob had the means to feed himself and so had fixed himself supper (Genesis 25:29). Esau ask Jacob for food (Genesis 25:30). Jacob took advantage of the situation and offered to trade the food for Esau's birthright. Being hungry and feeling faint, Esau agreed (Genesis 25:31-34). The birthright of the firstborn was of great value. When the father died, the firstborn not only became the leader of the family but received twice as much as his younger brothers did. Therefore, Esau traded the leadership and the associated riches of his position for a bowl of stew! When Isaac was dying he called for Esau and ask him to go and hunt a deer and prepare venison for him before he died, because he loved Esau's 'savory meat.' (Genesis 27:1-5) Isaac favored Esau and Rebekah favored Jacob (Genesis 25:28). Rebekah came up with a scheme to raise Jacob into the leadership of the family (Genesis 27:6-17). Remember, he already had the birthright, all he needed was the blessing. Jacob disguised himself as Esau and Rebekah prepared goat to taste like venison. Jacob took the food into Isaac and lied to his father to convince him that he was Esau (Genesis 27:22). Isaac ate the food and then blessed Jacob (Genesis 27:23,28,29). Soon after Esau returned with his offering, expecting a blessing (Genesis 27:30,31). Isaac realizing his mistake and how he was deceived, he shook with anger and told Esau that Jacob had stolen his blessing (Genesis 27:33-35). Esau was very angry at Jacob. Angry enough to kill (Genesis 27:36,41). Actually Jacob bought Esau's birthright and stole his blessing. Esau had every right to be angry!! However, He should be angry at himself for treating his position in the family so lightly that he would consider stew to be worth more than his duties to the family unit. Being a hunter, he should have been knowledgeable about the plants that were edible. He should have sustained himself in the field with 'nuts and berries.'

**Samson's wife given to another -** Samson, also suffered an injustice. He married a Philistine woman. She deceived him which angered him so much that he went home to his father's house. When he cooled down and returned to his wife he discovered that his father-in-law had given his wife to another, so Samson destroyed the Philistine's crops for revenge (Judges 14:1-4,7,15-20;15:1-5).

## Jealousy -

**Cain and Abel -** The story of Cain and Abel has a big question attached to it. For example, just when did God prescribe that sacrifices be offered or was it the idea of Cain and Abel to show worship to God? I can only assume that they were requested to do so. The scriptures state "in the process of time," indicating that a time was established and that Cain and Abel "brought" indicating that a place was assigned (Genesis 4:3,4). Therefore, we can conclude that a process was also prescribed. Abel brought the first born of his flock and must have butchered them because the scriptures state that he brought their fat (Genesis 4:4). Cain knew what was required and chose to ignore God's instructions. He wanted to do it his way! God knew that Cain did not have any animals to sacrifice. The solution would be for Cain to trade with Abel, the fruit of the ground for sheep and goats to sacrifice. From then until the crucifixion of Jesus, there has always been blood associated with sin offerings. Cain's anger proves that he knew that his offering was wrong and that he was caught trying to 'just get by.' (Genesis 4:5) His wroth overcame him and he probably said in himself, 'If God wants blood, I'll give Him blood!!!'" His next act was to offer the blood of his brother (Genesis 4:8). Being jealous of his brother and not obeying God were the sins that lead Cain from the presence of God (Genesis 4:12-14). My favorite verse in this whole passage is, "If thou doest well, shalt thou not be accepted? and if thou doest not well, sin lieth at the door. And unto thee shall be his desire, and thou shalt rule over him." (Genesis 4:7) Replace the word 'sin' with 'Satan' and you will clearly see what we have been struggling against since the beginning of time. Also, the reinforcement of the promise of man's position over Satan, "and thou shalt rule over him" (Genesis 3:15).

**Leah and Rachel** – Jacob ran from his brother, Esau's, anger because he had taken advantage of him twice in trading for his birthright and stealing Esau's blessing. As was noted earlier, Esau purposed to kill Jacob. He went to his uncle Laban's house in Haran. He met Rachel there and fell in love with her (Genesis 29:18,30). It was determined that Jacob would work for Laban seven years then be allowed to marry Rachel (Genesis 29:15-20). When the time had come for Jacob to receive his bride, his father-in-law sent Leah, the eldest sister, to Jacob instead of Rachel (Genesis 29:21-25). Leah being the oldest had to be married before the younger sister (Genesis 29:26). Laban struck another deal with Jacob to marry Rachel. Another seven years of servitude (Genesis 29:27,28). Leah and Rachel were daughters of a wealthy man and were used to being waited on. Laban gave them maids from his own staff to carry on this tradition. To Leah he gave Zilpah and Rachel he gave Bilhah (Genesis 29:24,29). Even though Jacob now had two wives, he loved Rachel more than Leah (Genesis 29:30). He wanted her in the first place!! God honored both marriages and seeing that Leah was mistreated, He "...opened her womb: but Rachel was barren." (Genesis 29:31). This would indicate that often they who are despised by men are favored by God. Leah gave birth to four boys, Rachel's jealousy got the better of her and she confronted Jacob. "And when Rachel saw that she bare Jacob no children, Rachel envied her sister; and said unto Jacob, Give me children, or else I die. And Jacob's anger was kindled against Rachel: and he said, Am I in God's stead, who hath withheld from thee the fruit of the womb?" (Genesis 30:1,2) Rachel was so intent on having children that she gave her maid to her husband to bare him children on her behalf (Genesis 30:3-8). A competition began between the sisters. Leah had stopped producing, so not to be out done, she gave her maid to Jacob (Genesis 30:9-13). I found it amusing that she named one of her sons 'Gad.' The Hebrew translation is troop or large company. Genesis 30:11 reads, "And Leah said, A troop cometh: and she called his name Gad." This being Jacobs's seventh son, this comment of Leah's could be translated in today's phrasing as, "It's on!!" When the sister's contest was over Jacob had twelve sons and one daughter. God uses our weakness's to bring about His plans. He had promised Abraham that his seed would be a mighty nation. Who would ever imagine that he would use Laban's duplicity, Rachel's jealousy and Leah's competitive natures to fulfill His plan. Basically it was jealousy that made Jacob's family so large!

**King Saul and David -** David went boldly in battle against the Philistine hero, Goliath and defeated him (1 Samuel 17:23-54). Saul was jealous of David because the people said that David was a better warrior than him (1 Samuel 18:7,8). The defeat of Goliath by a shepherd boy with just a sling and rock demoralized the Philistines. They turned and ran. The Israeli army was able to catch them and kill them. Not only was the Philistine army affected, but when the news was told back home the whole country was fearful. Therefore, the revelers had it right. Saul had killed his thousands and David his tens of thousands. The jealousy of David by Saul set up an artificial barrier between the king (Saul) and one of his most loyal subjects. Saul went on to try to kill or have David killed many times before his (Saul) death.

## Self-willed Disobedience –

Leah had a daughter by Jacob. Her name was Dinah (Genesis 30:21; 34:1). Being the only girl in the family, she was jealously guarded by her brothers. Jacob had left the land where Laban lived and settled in the land of the Hivites (Genesis 33:18-20; 34:2). Dinah was curious about the other girls in the area, so she left her dwelling and went to the city to make friends. Shechem, the prince of the land saw her he found her desirable and took her and defiled her (Genesis 34:2). He loved her and wanted her for his wife (Genesis 34:3.4). Her brothers were very angry that this evil thing had happened to her (Genesis 34:7). Hamor, Shechem's father, went to Jacob and arranged a marriage with Dinah and Shechem. Jacob agreed to the marriage as long as all the men be circumcised. Once this was done then they would take the Hivite women in marriage and the Hivite men could take the Jewish women in marriage and they would trade together and live in peace side by side (Genesis 34:6-24). This should have been the end of the matter. The sons of Jacob were so angry they had fostered deceit in their heart (Genesis 34:13). Simeon and Levi were more angry that the rest. When the Hivite men were recuperating from their surgeries, Simeon and Levi went into the city and killed them and took all their possessions (Genesis 34:25-29). Because Simeon and Levi were cruel in their anger, Jacob cursed them instead of blessing them on his death bed (Genesis 49:5-7). The passage reads, "Simeon and Levi are brethren; instruments of cruelty are in their habitations. O my soul, come not thou into their secret; unto their assembly, mine honour, be not thou united: for in their anger they slew a man, and in their self will they digged down a wall. Cursed be their anger, for it was fierce; and their wrath, for it was cruel: I will divide them in Jacob, and scatter them in Israel." They did not actually take a shovel and dig into a dirt wall. The phrase used here means that a deal was made and boundaries were set. A wall was erected, so to speak. These two men dishonored the agreement and ignored the "walls." While they had a right to be angry at the treatment of their sister, Jacob had resolved the matter and the offense was covered. Simeon's and Levi's response to Jacob's inquiry reveals their reason for their burning anger. "And they said, Should he deal with our sister as with an harlot?" (Genesis 34:31) While their indignation was righteous, their actions were self-willed and disobedient. It dishonored their father, and made him to be untrustworthy in his dealings in the eyes of the rest of the Hivites. Jacob also, feared retribution, "And Jacob said to Simeon and Levi, Ye have troubled me to make me to stink among the inhabitants of the land, among the Canaanites and the Perizzites: and I being few in number, they shall gather themselves together against me, and slay me; and I shall be destroyed, I and my house." (Genesis 34:30) Just a reminder that when we take matters into our own hands, we will always do more harm than good. Instead of solving the situation, most likely we will cause it to be prolonged.

## Other people's stubbornness -

The Lord prepares the way back to Him and a person to deliver the message (a prophet). We may not know the calling or the preparation of the person, but be assured that God has the situation under control. Who would have ever thought that the Hebrew baby hidden in the river would be raised as an Egyptian, flee to Midian and be sent by God again into Egypt to gain the release of the Hebrews? (Exodus 3:7-10) That's exactly what happened! Moses gathered all the elders and went to Pharaoh and did all that God had commanded. Pharaoh's heart being hardened refused to let the Israelites go. Pharaoh became so tired of dealing with Moses that he threw him out of his Palace under the threat of death (Exodus 10:28). Moses delivered the prophesy about the death of the firstborn of the Egyptians given to him by God (Exodus 11:1-8). Even after all the miracles that had been shown to Pharaoh, he still was a hardhearted non-believer. When Moses had delivered his message, it is said, "He went out from Pharaoh in a great anger" (Exodus 11:8), though he was the meekest of all the men of the earth. He probably expected that the very threat of the death of the firstborn would have convinced Pharaoh to comply, especially as Pharaoh had complied so far, and seen how exactly all Moses's predictions were fulfilled. But it did not have that effect, Pharaoh's proud heart would not yield, not even to save all the firstborn of his kingdom. It is no wonder that men are not turned away from their evil ways by the prospects of eternal misery in hell, when the prospect of the loss of all that is dear to them in this world will not convince them. Moses was provoked to a holy indignation, being grieved for the hardness of Pharaoh's heart. To be angry at sin is the best way not to sin in anger. Remember, "Be ye angry, and sin not: let not the sun go down upon your wrath: neither give place to the devil. (Ephesians 4:26,27) Any occasion of sin will allow the devil to enter your life. Anger is the largest door you can give him. When you get angry you no longer care about who's around, who hears you or your personal character. Satan can walk right in and get comfortable.

## Impatience and Idolatry -

Pharaoh finally relented and sent the Israelites away. Then changed his mind and chased them down with his army with the intent to bring them back into captivity or kill them. He would have been happy either way. We all know that story and how it comes out. The people were told to borrow the precious metals and fine clothes from their Egyptian neighbors and friends. The Hebrew people obeyed God and took the silver and gold and fine clothes and thereby looting or spoiling the country (Exodus 12:35,36). They carried the spoils with them as they went. God led them to mount Sinai where they camped (Exodus 19:1,2). Moses was called up to the mount by God (Exodus 19:20). He received the stone tablets with the Ten Commandments (Exodus 31:18). God also, gave him instructions for the construction of the tabernacle, the Priest's clothes and all the utensils to be used in the service of the Lord. God also laid out other laws and ordinances for the conduct of the people as a community. The whole record is included in eleven chapters (Exodus 20-31). Therefore, it is logical to assume that Moses was with God for an extended period of time. The people, not knowing what had happened to Moses, only that he was "delayed," looked for another god to lead them (Exodus 32:1). They were an insecure and impatient people. Their impatience made them turn to a god they could see...the golden calf (Exodus 32:1-6). They used the gold and silver from Egypt to make the calf. God had intended that the gold and silver be used to make the utensils for the tabernacle. The people made an idol, and insult, not to mention an abomination to God. When Moses saw the idol he became enraged. Moses became so angry at the impatience and idolatry of the people that he threw the tablets and broke them (Exodus 32:19). Then he destroyed the molten calf and scattered the dust of the precious metals (Exodus 32:20). The Hebrew people wasted all that God had supplied for them. Are we doing the same thing?

## Complaining and dissatisfaction with God's provisions –

The Israelites complained to Moses about the manna that God had provided. Their thoughts had went back to Egypt and the variety of foods they had access to. The people lusted for meat and complained to Moses. He had no way to provide that, the manna came from God. He could not feed the people anything. Moses was so burdened by the peoples constant complaints that he ask God to kill him (Numbers 11:10-15). God was angry at the complainers, too. We discussed this in the last chapter. The Lord provided the meat that they cried for. God sent them quails for 30 days (Numbers 11:18-23, 31,32). They ate all the meat they wanted, but some paid a high price for the privilege. God sent a plague into the camp and killed the leaders of the complainers (Numbers 11:33,34).

## The burden of responsibility –

Moses became overwhelmed with the responsibility of leadership and complained to God (Numbers 11:11-15). Leading the nation of Israel was a daunting task. It has been estimated that about one million people left Egypt (counting men, women and children, not to mention the flocks of sheep, goats and cattle). God listened to Moses and determined to get him help. The Lord sanctified seventy men to help Moses (Numbers 11:16,17, 24-30). He must have had a big job, if it took that many men to help him! Moses was so overwhelmed with his responsibilities that he actually lost his composure to God. Have you ever been so fed up with a situation that your prayers sound more like a complaint? Moses's prayer was this, "And Moses said unto the LORD, Wherefore hast thou afflicted thy servant? and wherefore have I not found favor in thy sight, that thou laid the burden of all this people upon me? Have I conceived all this people? have I begotten them, that thou should say unto me, Carry them in thy bosom, as a nursing father bears the sucking child, unto the land which thou swore unto their fathers? Whence should I have flesh to give unto all this people? for they weep unto me, saying, Give us flesh, that we may eat. I am not able to bear all this people alone, because it is too heavy for me. And if thou deal thus with me, kill me, I pray thee, out of hand, if I have found favor in thy sight; and let me not see my wretchedness." (Numbers 11:11-15)

## Disobedience –

**The manna kept overnight** – The Israelites were commanded by God through Moses to eat all the manna they gathered. To gather only what is prescribed for each person living with them. One omer (about 5.1 pints) per person (Exodus 16:16). All that was gathered was to be consumed that day, none was to be saved for the next day, except for the gathering for the holy sabbath (Exodus 16:19,22-26). As you might have figured, some decided to save a portion for the morning (Exodus 16:20). Manna is unstable and if left overnight it stinks and draws worms, it fell with the dew early in the morning and when the sun was fully up, the manna melted away (Exodus 16:20,21). Moses became angry at the people that disobeyed God's instructions. The window for gathering was just a few hours so if you wanted your daily portion you had better not sleep in!

**The sacrifice of the goat** – The sacrifice of the sin offering was meant to be propitiatory, meaning, it was offered to win the favor of, and bring the person who offered it into good standing with God. This was usually a female goat for the common people (Leviticus 4:27,28) and a young bull for the congregation (Leviticus 4:13,14). A sin offering was required even if the person sinned unintentionally (Leviticus 4:2). The sons of Aaron that were trained to help him with the sacrifices were killed by God because they brought 'strange fire' into the tabernacle (Leviticus 10:1,2). The replacements, Eleazar and Ithamar, were thrown into service at the last minute with basic instructions (Leviticus 10:12-15). On this occasion the priests were offering a sin sacrifice for the whole congregation. Moses had instructed a goat be sacrificed for the sin of the congregation instead of the bullock (Leviticus 9:15). When he inquired about the sacrifice, he discovered the goat was completely burnt as would have been done with a sin offering for the common people. Sacrificing a goat in lieu was a complete deviation from the routine. The law of the sin offerings; the blood was brought into the holy place, like the sin offerings for the priest, then the flesh was to be burnt outside the camp in a clean place, or it was to be eaten by the priest in the holy place (Leviticus 6:30). The reason this was done is because the priests were to bear the iniquity of the congregation (Leviticus 10:17). Now the blood of this goat was not brought into the holy place, and yet, it seems, it was burnt outside of the camp. Notice the gentle scolding Moses gives to Aaron and his sons for this irregularity. Here again Aaron sons are said to be those that were left alive (Leviticus 10:16). You would have thought that they would have taken warning knowing their brothers were killed by God for a ritualistic infraction. Moses was angry with them for their transgression. Though he was the meekest man in the world, it seems he could be angry, and when he thought God was disobeyed and dishonored, and the priesthood endangered, he would be angry. Yet observe how very mildly he deals with Aaron and his sons, considering their present affliction. He only tells them they should indeed have eaten it in the holy place, but is willing to hear what they have to say for themselves, being reluctant to speak against them because of their grief for their loved ones. Moses charged the fault upon Eleazar and Ithamar, but it is most likely that they did what Aaron told them, and therefore he, Aaron, apologized for the trespass. He might have pleaded that this was a sin offering for the congregation, and if it had been a bullock it must have been wholly burnt (Leviticus 4:21). Therefore, why not the same procedure even though it was a goat? But it seems it was otherwise ordered at this time, and therefore he makes his grief his excuse. He speaks of his grief, such things have befallen me, such sad things, which could not but go near his heart, and make it very happy. He was a high priest taken from among men, and could not put off natural affection when he put on the holy garments. He held his peace, yet his sorrow was stirred (Leviticus 10:3). He makes this an excuse for his error in the handling of the sin offering. He could not have eaten it because he was in mourning and with a sorrowful spirit and would this have been accepted? He does not plead that his heart was so full of grief that he had no appetite for it, but that he feared it would not be accepted. Acceptance with God is the great thing we should desire and aim at in all our religious services, particularly in the Lord's Supper, which is our eating of the sin offering. The humanly sorrow is a very great hindrance to our acceptable performance of our holy duties. It is disorienting to ourselves, takes our joy and makes us heavyhearted and it is displeasing to God, whose will it is that we should serve him cheerfully (Deuteronomy 12:7). "They shall not offer wine offerings to the LORD, neither shall they be pleasing unto him: their sacrifices shall be unto them as the bread of mourners; all that eat thereof shall be polluted: for their bread for their soul shall not come into the house of the LORD." (Hosea 9:4)

**Balaam goes with the princes of Moab** - Balaam misunderstood God's instructions concerning his traveling with the princes of Moab. Balak (the king of Moab, Numbers 22:4) had sent messengers to Balaam before (Numbers 22:5) and God had told Balaam not to go to Moab with them (Numbers 22:13). Balak sent princes of land to him to make the same request (Numbers 22:15). When Balaam inquired again of God, He told him to go, only under certain circumstances. "And God came unto Balaam at night, and said unto him, If the men come to call thee, rise up, and go with them; but yet the word which I shall say unto thee, that shalt thou do. And Balaam rose up in the morning, and saddled his ass, and went with the princes of Moab." (Numbers 22:20,21) Balaam did not wait for the men to call him! He disobeyed the Lord's instructions. How often do we act under our own understanding when we do not pay close attention to God's instructions because we do not study the Bible, pray or fast as often as we should. Therefore, we do not hear God clearly and do that which we believe to be of God and totally mess it up. God intended to stop Balaam from going where He told him not to go. He placed an angel in his path (Numbers 22:22). Balaam did not see the angel of the Lord, but his ass did (Numbers 22:23). The animal tried to save Balaam's life by turning away from the angel. She did this three times and every time Balaam would beat her with a stick (Numbers 22:23-27). God caused the animal to speak and plead her case (Numbers 22:28-30). Then God allowed Balaam to see the angel. When the angel defensed the ass, Balaam understood the error of his ways and offered to return home (Numbers 22:31-34). There are two examples of disobedience in this story. The obvious one is the ass turning off the path set for it by Balaam. She was of course, punished by her master for her perceived disobedience. We have the more subtle example of Balaam assuming that God wanted him to go to Moab. Disobedience will always lead us into great trouble.

**The idolatry of the Israelites** -The Israelites, having just come from Egypt, stayed for a while in the land of Midian. They were there long enough for the women to seduce some of the Israeli men into worshiping their god, Baal (Numbers 31:16). Of course, this greatly angered God! Remember, "I am the LORD thy God, which have brought thee out of the land of Egypt, out of the house of bondage. Thou shalt have no other gods before me." (Exodus 20:2,3) Some of the people must have forgotten! Moses was instructed to declare war on the Midianites to cleanse the people of their sins and temptation. This meant kill all and take no spoils. The leaders of the warring party brought back women, children and their livestock (Numbers 31:9,11,12). That made Moses very angry (Numbers 31:14). They were given instructions on how to correct the situation (Numbers 31:15-18). "Now therefore kill every male among the little ones, and kill every woman that hath known man by lying with him." (Numbers 31:17) They were the most likely to have seduced those men who fell away to sin by idolatry.

**Queen Vashti's rebellion** –Ahasuerus (the Greek version is Xerxes), king of the Medo-Persian Kingdom, his rule extended from India to Ethiopia and contained 127 provinces (Esther 1:1). In the third year of his reign he called all his nobles and princes together and threw a feast that lasted 180 days (Esther 1:3,4). It is thought that this was a war planning meeting to expand his influence into Greece. The battle immortalized by the movie '300'. Where 300 Greek warriors held the whole Persian army at bay for an extended period of time. The Greeks were eventually defeated. During this feast, he showed his guests the riches of his kingdom to assure them that he was powerful enough to win any war they would wage. After the 180 day feast, he threw a seven day feast for his subjects (Esther 1:5-9). One of the things he considered to be his 'riches' was his queen, Vashti. He summoned her to appear before him and all his friends, to show her off (Esther 1:10). She refused to appear because it was against Persian etiquette as well as to female propriety. Her refusal angered him so much that he divorced her (Esther 1:10-15, 19). The men were afraid that the show of independence and disrespect of Vashti would infect the women of the kingdom when they heard of it and they would disrespect their husbands like the queen did (Esther 1:16-18,20-22). Ahasuerus actually overreacted in his drunk and proud condition. He was angry that his queen did not come running when he beckoned her. Even more important, he was embarrassed that his power was thwarted by a mere woman. I guess the divorce decree read, 'on the grounds of a wounded pride.'

**Shadrach, Meshach, and Abednego's stand against Nebuchadnezar** – Nebuchadnezar made an image of gold and commanded everyone to bow down and worship it when music was played (Daniel 3:1-7). Whosoever did not obey was to be cast into a fiery furnace (Daniel 3:6). Shadrach, Meshach, and

Abednego refused to worship any other God but the God of Israel. Nebuchadnezar was told of their disobedience and became enraged (Daniel 3:8-13). When they were questioned, they told him that they would never worship any other God but theirs (Daniel 3:14-18). Nebuchadnezar became enraged and the three were tied and thrown into the furnace after the heat was turned up to seven times its normal operating temperature (Daniel 3:19-21). We all know what happened. God sent an angel to save them (Daniel 3:24-27). God showed all those around that He was the one and only God. Even the king, Nebuchadnezar, believed and decreed that the God of Israel was to be honored (Daniel 3:28,29). Do you believe in God enough to face a fiery furnace?

## Betrayal -

**The false accusation of Joseph -** Joseph was sold by his brothers because they were jealous of their father's attention and affection for him (Genesis 37:11,22-28). He was taken to Egypt and sold as a slave to the captain of Pharaoh's guards, Potiphar (Genesis 39:1). Joseph's master saw that the Lord was with him and he was successful in all that he did. He put Joseph in charge of his whole house (Genesis 39:2-6). Potiphar's wife was attracted to Joseph and constantly tried to seduce him but Joseph always refused her (Genesis 39:7-12). One such occasion, he had to leave his coat behind to flee from her and escape her clutches (Genesis 39:12). Her disappointment caused her to be angry and scheme against Joseph. She accused him of attempted rape (Genesis 39:13-18). Joseph's master believed his wife and felt betrayed by Joseph. He had trusted him with all that he had, except, of course his wife. She had his coat as proof. What more evidence did he need? Potiphar became angry and put Joseph in prison (Genesis 39:19,20).

**Balak felt betrayed by Balaam -** Balak heard rumors of the conquests of Israel as they came out of Egypt. Now they were camped close to him and he was afraid (Numbers 22:1-4). He sent an envoy to retrieve Balaam to curse Israel. We discussed this in the previous section. Remember, God initially told Balaam not to go to Balak, but he eventually went. Balak wanted Balaam to curse the Israelites so that he could defeat them and drive them away from his kingdom (Numbers 22:6). God's blessed people cannot be cursed (Numbers 22:12). Balak was happy to see Balaam when he arrived and took him up to see the extent of the people (Numbers 22:41). Balaam told Balak many times that he would not say or do anything that God had not told him, but he did not listen. He took the seer three different places to see and perhaps curse the Israelites. Each time, in every place, Balaam blessed the people and did not curse them. Balak felt betrayed and was angry. He sent Balaam away, harshly (Numbers 24:10,11). Balaam once again, told Balak that he did just what he told him he would do (Numbers 24:12,13). Balaam's declaration should be every believer's and spoken by us continually. Balaam declared, "...I cannot go beyond the commandment of the LORD, to do either good or bad of mine own mind; but what the LORD saith, that will I speak?" (Numbers 24:13) How much better would our lives be if that which came out of our mouths would be what the LORD says!

**Sampson betrayed by his wife -** Sampson went into the land of the Philistine's. They were the enemy of Israel since Israel came out of Egypt. While he was there, he saw a young woman to whom he was attracted and wanted to make his wife (Judges 14:1-3). While in route to arrange the marriage he was attacked by a lion. Sampson slew the lion and he continued on his journey (Judges 14:5,6). When he was in route to the wedding, he turned off the main road and went to look at the carcass of the lion. Bees had built their hive in it. Sampson took a handful of the honey and returned to the road to meet his parents. He shared some of the honey with them (Judges 14:8,9). Sampson never told anyone about the lion and the bees. During the wedding feast, he posed a riddle with a bet that if his companions could solve the riddle he would give them each a change of garments (Judges 14:12). If they could not solve the riddle they were to all give him a change of garments. A simple bet for a clever riddle. The men pondered. Thought and argued it out, but could not discover the answer. Since they had not figured out the solution to the riddle, they turned to Sampson's bride, they were her countrymen and Sampson was just a Israelite. The enemy after all! They went as far as to threatened her family with grievous harm (Judges 14:15). She nagged Sampson until he told her the story of the lion and the bees. She then told it to the guests of the wedding feast (Judges 14:16,17). When the guests came to Sampson with the solution to the riddle, he became angry at the betrayal of his wife (Judges 14:18). He paid off his debt and went to his father's house in anger to sulk, over the deceitfulness of the Philistines and his wife (Judges 14:19).

## False Sense of Pride -

The Midianites, Amalekites and children from the east (probably the armies of Jordan) had assembled themselves against Israel (Judges 6:33). Gideon gathered an army to oppose them (Judges 6:35). The LORD was with Gideon and his army so they prevailed against their enemy. While the enemy was fleeing, Gideon sent messengers to Ephraim with instructions to them to cut off the enemies escape at the river. They obeyed and captured two princes of the Midianites. The Ephramites killed the princes and brought the heads to Gideon (Judges 7:25). This was an indication that they considered him their leader. The Ephraimites, when they brought the heads of Oreb and Zeeb to Gideon as general, instead of congratulating him upon his successes and addressing him with thanks for his great services, as they ought to have done, picked a quarrel with him which became very heated. Their accusation was very peevish and unreasonable: "Why hast thou served us thus, that thou calledst us not, when thou wentest to fight with the Midianites? And they did chide with him sharply." (Judges 8:1). Ephraim was brother to Manasseh, Gideon's tribe, and had the per-eminence in Jacob's blessing and in Moses's, and therefore was very jealous of Manasseh, lest that tribe should at any time eclipse the honor of theirs. Hence we find 'Manasseh against Ephraim and Ephraim against Manasseh' (Isaiah 9:21). Gideon soothed their hurt feelings by reminding them that they had done the deed that would be remembered through Israel for eternity. That is: captured and killed the princes (Judges 8:2,3). This is also a story to prove Proverbs 15:1, "A soft answer turneth away wrath: but grievous words stir up anger." Gideon could have said something like this was a small matter and we did not think we needed your help, thus escalating the disagreement. He chose to quell the Ephraimites by quietly proving to them that they had gained the lion's share of the glory by their late entry into the battle.

## Insolence and Inconsiderate Attitude –

The city of Jabesh-Gilead was besieged by the Ammonites. The elders of the city were afraid so they tried to make a treaty with the enemy (1 Samuel 11:1). The general of the Ammonites agreed under the condition that he could blind their right eyes (1 Samuel 11:2). This would make them unfit for military service. They ask for seven days to consider the proposal (1 Samuel 11:3). They sent messengers to every corner of the country to seek for help (1 Samuel 11:3). When the messengers came to Gibeah (the city of Saul), the citizens wept, and when Saul heard the news the Spirit of God came upon him and he became angry (1 Samuel 11:4-6). Saul was angry at the insolence of the Ammonites, angry at the cowardice and sneaking spirit of the men of Jabesh-Gilead, angry that they had not sent him notice sooner of the Ammonites' arrival and the peril they were likely to be subjected to. He was, also, angry to see his neighbors weeping, when it would have been better for them to be preparing for war. Saul gathered an army, went to Jabesh-Gilead, and defeated the Ammonites so bad that when they broke ranks and scattered there was not two of them that traveled together (1 Samuel 11:7-11). If God is our king, then doesn't it make sense to call on our king for help when troubles and enemies come? We should give all our situations to God. Give Him the bad and give Him the good. It is He that allowed the bad to come upon you and it is He that supplies the good. "Ye that fear the LORD, trust in the LORD: he is their help and their shield." (Psalms 115:11)

## Presumptive Attitude of Youth –

Israel and the Philistines had been enemies for generations. We discussed this fact before. There was always war or some sort of animosity between these two countries. This particular time they were at war and set in battle formation against one another (1 Samuel 17:21). David, a little shepherd boy, went to the front to bring his brothers food and check on the battle situation for his father (1 Samuel 17:20,22). While he was there, Goliath came out and taunted Israel (1 Samuel 17:23). Eliab, David's older brother, had been at war with the Philistines at least forty days. Goliath had mocked Israel and shamed them into a stalemate daily (1 Samuel 17:23,24). When David heard the speech of Goliath, he became angry and spoke against Goliath. He put the army to shame referring to Goliath as an 'uncircumcised Philistine' and reminded them that they were 'the army of the living God'. The army was blessed by God and their king was anointed of God and there they stood, afraid of one oversized man. Isn't that what we do? Look at the size of the problem instead of trusting in the power of God. Eliab, being the oldest, was ashamed when David presumed (in Eliab's eyes) to be braver and stronger than the whole army. Eliab became angry at David accusing him of being proud and naughty. "I know thy pride, and the naughtiness of thine heart; for thou art come down that thou mightest see the battle." (1 Samuel 17:28). We all know the rest of this story. David knew that God was with them and acted upon that knowledge.

## Treachery -

Saul became jealous of David because the people favored David over him. When Saul and David lead the army home after a battle against the Philistines, the women sang praises to them. They credited Saul with killing thousands and David with tens of thousands (1 Samuel 18:6,7). This made Saul very angry and he mistrusted David after that (1 Samuel 18:8,9). He made himself an enemy of David's (1 Samuel 18:29). Jonathan, Saul's son was best friends with David and loved him like a brother (1 Samuel 18:1,3,4). Saul had determined that David must die to save his legacy (1 Samuel 18:25;19:1,2). Jonathan was put in the middle of the situation and had to choose who he would support. He chose David (1 Samuel 19:2,4; 20:4). Saul was angry with Jonathan because he betrayed his family and turned his back on his father, therefore dealt treacherously with Saul. Saul was so angry with Jonathan that he tried to kill him with a spear (1 Samuel 20:30-33).

## Shame -

Jonathan, finally realizing that Saul meant to do David real harm became extremely angry at his father that he left the feast without eating (1 Samuel 20:34). Jonathan was ashamed of Saul for wanting to kill David when he had done nothing wrong (1 Samuel 20:32). Also, he was ashamed of himself because he did not recognize that Saul intended to do David harm (1 Samuel 20:33). Divided loyalties will always bring shame and confusion!

**Rachel stole her father's idols -** Jacob was the nephew of Laban and had been sent to live with him by his mother after he and she had tricked Isaac, his father, into giving Esau's blessing to Jacob (Genesis 27; 28:1-5). Laban dealt dishonorably with him in that he made him work seven years for the daughter he loved only to be given the other and had to work seven additional years to receive the woman he truly desired (Genesis 29:18-27). That was fourteen years of free labor Laban got out of Jacob. Every time Jacob tried to leave and go back to his father's house, Laban would come up with some kind of scheme to keep him there. God blessed Jacob and by extension, Laban was blessed (Genesis 30:25-32). After twenty years of this kind of treatment, Jacob decided that Laban would never let him go with his blessings (Genesis 30:25-32; 31:38). He gathered his family and possessions then left when Laban went into the field (Genesis 31:17-21). Rachel took her father's idols (Genesis 31:19). The idols were significant because they not only were thought to be the protectors and the blessings of the house, but the possession of the father-in-laws idols by the son-in-law was proof that the son-in-law was the principle heir. Therefore, Rachel robbed the sons of Laban of their rightful inheritance. Rachel and Leah were not very happy with the way Laban had handled his affairs on their account. They had no inheritance from him since they were females and expected to marry their wealth (Genesis 31:14-16). Laban was angry with Jacob because Rachel had stolen her father's idols. He chased him down to retrieve his possessions. Jacob was not aware of the indiscretion of Rachel. Jacob was angry with Laban because he chased him down and accused him of theft and impropriety. This fulfilled the blessing that Isaac bestowed upon Jacob when he left home to go to live with Laban (Genesis 28:4). "And give thee the blessing of Abraham, to thee, and to thy seed with thee; that thou mayest inherit the land wherein thou art a stranger, which God gave unto Abraham."

**The retrieving of the Levitical priest -** There is no better way to begin this discussion than to quote the Bible concerning the times involved. "In those days there was no king in Israel, but every man did that which was right in his own eyes." (Judges 17:6) There was no central meeting place. The temple had not been built in Jerusalem and the location of the tabernacle was not mentioned. Therefore, every man made a place for himself to worship (Judges 17:5). An Ephraimite, named Micah, had done just that. He had turned his house into a house of gods. He had in his house a carved image and a cast image (Judges 17:5). Not being satisfied with idolatry he made pieces of the priestly wardrobe, the ephod. This was to be worn only by the high priest. Micah, also, hired a Levitical priest to be his spiritual adviser (Judges 17:7-13). With all the 'bases covered', Micah thought he had a good handle on the 'god thing'. There were men of the tribe of Dan spying out the land because Israel had not totally settled into the promised land (Judges 18:1,2). These were men that followed Mosaic law and when they heard and recognized the priests voice and saw the religious items in Micah's house, they knew they had to destroy the idols and retrieve the priest (Judges 18:14). See also Deuteronomy 13:12-18. That is just what they did! The immediate effect on the city was to destroy the local place of worship (Judges 18:22-24). The men of the city became angry and chased after the Danites to retrieve their property. When the Ephraimites realized that the Danites were stronger than them, they returned to their homes (Judges 18:25,26). Idolatry and false religions cannot be made acceptable by mixing it with God's ordered rituals. WRONG IS ALWAYS WRONG!!!

## Disappointment -

**Ahab and the acquisition of the vineyard -** Ahab was the king of Israel and his palace was next to a vineyard owned by a man named Naboth. Ahab tried to acquire the property but

Naboth would not sell. Ahab became angry and went into his bed chamber to pouted. He even refused to eat. (1 Kings 21:1-4) What a childish reaction for anyone when faced with disappointment, let alone a king!

**Naaman the Syrian leper** - Naaman was the captain of the Syrian army, a brave and powerful man. He was a leper. (2 Kings 5:1) The Syrians had conquered Israel and a young girl had been given to Naaman's wife as maid (2 Kings 5:2). She had told her mistress about the great prophet in Israel that would cure her husband of his leprosy (2 Kings 5:3). Naaman received permission from the king of Syria to go to Israel to inquire of the great prophet for delivery from the leprosy (2 Kings 5:4,5). Naaman took his whole entourage to Elisha's (the prophet) house (2 Kings 5:9). Being a man of God, he already heard from God and knew what Naaman had to do to be healed. He sent a servant out to meet Naaman to give him God's instructions (2 Kings 5:10). Naaman was angry at Elisha because he did not come out of his house to see him and pray publicly for him. He expected a big show, a gigantic display of God's awesome power and might (2 Kings 5:11). Naaman was told, by a servant none the less, to wash himself seven times in the Jordan river. No great miracle! No great feat! No big deal! There were rivers in his country that he could bathe in, if that was all that it took to be healed! (2 Kings 5:12). Don't you just know that when he left Elisha's house that he was steaming mad. The servants of Naaman calmed him and convinced him to do as Elisha had directed (2 Kings 5:13). When he went to the Jordan river and dipped himself seven times, his leprosy was healed (2 Kings 5:14). God does not do His work with great fanfare, flashes of lightening and booming thunder. He quietly and effectively does what needs to be done. The lack of ceremony and show made Naaman think that there was to be no miraculous deed done on his behalf. He was extremely disappointed, after the big build up by his wife's maid and then gaining permission from his king to go. His hope and expectations were high. Then he was told, not even by the one who was supposed to heal him, to go for a swim in a dirty river. Insult on top of insult! Anyone with more faith in man than in God will be disappointed with life on this planet!

## Loss in a business deal –

The kingdom of Israel was divided for many years. The tribes in the north part of the country called themselves Israel and the tribes in the south referred to themselves as Judah. They often fought among themselves, and just about as often, joined forces to defeat a common enemy. Amaziah was the king in Judah at this time. He had determined to reunite Edom to the country. Edom had broken away from Judah many years before. Amaziah took a count of his own men and he had 300,000 ready for war, he hired 100,000 warriors from Israel to help him for one hundred pieces of silver (2 Chronicles 25:5,6). 400,000 good strong warriors should be enough to bring Edom back into submission. A man of God (a prophet) warned Amaziah that Israel was not to go into battle with him. God was not with Israel as He was with Judah (2 Chronicles 25:7). So, Amaziah sent the Israelites back home. The one hundred pieces of silver was a down payment to the men of Israel as they had planned to get rich from the spoils of war. They were very angry when they were released and they took their vengeance out on Judah and killed and looted their way back to their own country (2 Chronicles 25:10,13).

## Working all your life and having nothing –

Men and women are born into this world, raised and taught by their parents. Then they leave their homes to make a life for themselves. They will work, marry and have children, raise and teach them, so the cycle continues. This is God's plan and the children are the riches of a life of service to God. When earthly riches (gold, silver, property and possessions) become the focus of a person's life and labor. he is totally wasting his efforts. I cannot state this fact better than the Bible does. "But those riches perish by evil travail: and he begetteth a son, and there is nothing in his hand. As he came forth of his mother's womb, naked shall he return to go as he came, and shall take nothing of his labour, which he may carry away in his hand." (Ecclesiastes 5:14,15) Many people complain, "I have worked all my life and have nothing to show for it!" Solomon says in Ecclesiastes, you're working in the wrong place and for the wrong reasons and expecting the wrong reward. Working for earthly riches will be left behind when you die. Again the Bible says it best, "And this also is a sore evil, that in all points as he came, so shall he go: and what profit hath he that hath laboured for the wind? All his days also he eateth in darkness, and he hath much sorrow and wrath with his sickness." (Ecclesiastes 5:14-17) Working for God does not necessarily pay well on earth, but your reward is waiting for you when you get to heaven. Jesus admonishes us, "Lay not up for yourselves treasures upon earth, where moth and rust doth corrupt, and where thieves break through and steal: But lay up for yourselves treasures in heaven, where neither moth nor rust doth corrupt, and where thieves do not break through nor steal" (Matthew 6:19,20) MAD OR GLAD? It's truly your choice!

### To appear to be a false prophet –

Jonah was scared to go to Nineveh. He had good reason to be frightened. The ancients would test the prophet's words and if there was ever a time when they were not 100% accurate they would be stoned to death for being a false prophet. Jonah said that he knew that God would save the city. "...for I knew that thou art a gracious God, and merciful, slow to anger, and of great kindness, and repentest thee of the evil." (Jonah 4:2) He should have been happy that the people believed him and repented, but instead he became angry. I believe that he was scared that the people would consider him a false prophet because the city would not be destroyed in forty days as God had instructed him to prophesy (Jonah 3:1). Actually this was the greatest revival in the history of the world. The whole city turned from their evil ways and turned to God (Jonah 3:8). Jonah did not want to be there anyway, so when destruction did not come, he looked like a liar (speaking from a human perspective). Jonah had developed an attitude and left the city to pout (Jonah 4:5). God raised up a plant to shade him and protect him from the sun (Jonah 4:6). Although, he was glad for the plant, the Bible doesn't say Jonah thanked God for it. But he was upset when it died (Jonah 4:9). God had dealt with Nineveh, now He had to deal with Jonah. He ran away from the city and found himself a vantage point to watch the coming destruction (Jonah 4:5). When Jonah became displeased that the plant God gave him for shade had died, the LORD used the occasion to teach Jonah a lesson about mercy. "Then said the LORD, Thou hast had pity on the gourd, for the which thou hast not laboured, neither madest it grow; which came up in a night, and perished in a night: And should not I spare Nineveh, that great city, wherein are more than sixscore thousand persons that cannot discern between their right hand and their left hand; and also much cattle?" (Jonah 4:10,11) Are the souls of men not worth as much as a gourd? God's people today are a lot like Jonah. We are often more concerned about the material benefits so freely bestowed upon us by God than about the destiny of a lost world.

## Fear -

Joseph's brothers had sold him into slavery and he ended up in Egypt. Earlier in this book it was mentioned that Potiphar had Joseph put in prison under false pretenses (Genesis 39:7-

20). Joseph was brought out of prison and into the kings house because he could interpret dreams (Genesis 41:1-36). The king was so pleased that he made Joseph second in charge only to himself (Genesis 41:37-44). Joseph's brothers did not really know or care what became of him. They thought he might be dead. There came a famine in the land where Isaac and his sons lived. They had to travel to Egypt to buy grain for food. That meant dealing with Joseph. The first time they saw Joseph, they did not recognize him. The next time his brothers came to buy grain Joseph revealed himself to them and they were afraid that he was going to seek revenge on them for how they had treated him. The Bible says, "...And his brethren could not answer him; for they were troubled at his presence." (Genesis 45:3) Joseph comforted them by introducing himself to them, "And Joseph said unto his brethren, Come near to me, I pray you. And they came near. And he said, I am Joseph your brother, whom ye sold into Egypt. Now therefore be not grieved, nor angry with yourselves, that ye sold me hither: for God did send me before you to preserve life." (Genesis 45:4,5) Not all the bad things that happen to you are meant for your destruction or punishment. "...for God did send me before you to preserve life."

## Political power grab –

David's son Absalom had revolted against his father intending to be king himself. Of course, this caused a war between the followers of David and the followers of Absalom. David's side won the battle and Absalom was killed. Israel was a divided kingdom at this time, the northern ten tribes called themselves Israel and the southern two tribes were known as Judah. Judah decided that David must be returned to Jerusalem to rule from there as before (2 Samuel 19:11-15). There was no one sent to Israel to ask their opinion (2 Samuel 19:43). Israel figured that they were more important than Judah because they were comprised of ten of the twelve tribes and Judah was comprised of two. Therefore, by their reasoning, they had six times more say in the nation's business and by extension, the welfare and restoration of the king. The Bible states this best, "And the men of Israel answered the men of Judah, and said, We have ten parts in the king, and we have also more right in David than ye: why then did ye despise us, that our advice should not be first had in bringing back our king?" (2 Samuel 19:43) The men of Israel thought that the men of Judah were trying to take total control of the kingdom by being the only ones to have access to the king. This was far from the truth! David was from the area of Judah and the people considered him a close relative (2 Samuel 19:42). When power is involved great rivalries are formed by wicked men. Evils are seen to exist where none truly are.

## Oppression of God's people –

Israel was in captivity in Persia under king Artaxerxes. He allowed a small group of people to return to Jerusalem to repair the city walls. There were some Israelites that were never taken captive. There was a tribute that had to be paid to Persia though. Think of this as a tax (Nehemiah 5:4). Most of the people left behind were poor, the princes and most learned were taken to Persia to serve that king. There were not many jobs available since all the money had went to Persia. From the time of the captivity until the time of Nehemiah's return, the Jews had to survive the best way they could. Those who had no money hired themselves to those who had the land to gather their grain. They were paid in grain (Nehemiah 5:2). There was a famine, also, at that time, and those with land but not much money mortgaged their property to buy food (Nehemiah 5:3). The times were tough for those left behind and the only place to get money to buy food or pay the tribute was to borrow it from their wealthier brethren. Those who loaned the money used the land as mortgage collateral and charged usury (interest) (Nehemiah 5:3-5,10). By the time Nehemiah returned from Persia most of the people had nothing more to sell. The lenders had all their money and lands (Nehemiah 5:5). The fact that the wealthiest people had a strangle hold on their brethren made Nehemiah angry (Nehemiah 5:6). The charging of interest was forbidden by God when loans were made to fellow Jews. "If thou lend money to any of my people that is poor by thee, thou shalt not be to him as an usurer, neither shalt thou lay upon him usury." (Exodus 22:25) Nehemiah called an assembly and made the lenders honor God's law and return to the borrowers that which was due to them (Nehemiah 5:7,11,12). He set the priests as the spiritual watchdogs over them as they should have been from the beginning (Nehemiah 5:12).

## Deceit -

**Nebuchadnezzar's dream -** Nebuchadnezzar had a dream that bothered him so much that it woke him from his sleep (Daniel 2:1). He called his magicians, and astrologers, and sorcerers, and the Chaldeans (reputed to be the wisest men of ancient times) to tell him his dreams (Daniel 2:2). Nebuchadnezzar, the king, had forgotten the dream but it affected him so much that he desired the interpretation. The Chaldeans (wise men) ask the king to relate the dream (Daniel 2:4). "The king answered and said to the Chaldeans, The thing is gone from me: if ye will not make known unto me the dream, with the interpretation thereof, ye shall be cut in pieces, and your houses shall be made a dunghill. But if ye show the dream, and the interpretation thereof, ye shall receive of me gifts and rewards and great honour: therefore show me the dream, and the interpretation thereof." (Daniel 2:5,6) Nebuchadnezzar did not really trust his wise men. "But if ye will not make known unto me the dream, there is but one decree for you: for ye have prepared lying and corrupt words to speak before me, till the time be changed: therefore tell me the dream, and I shall know that ye can show me the interpretation thereof." (Daniel 2:9). The wise men told the king that no man on earth could do what he was asking of them, except the gods, and they did not live among the people (Daniel 2:10,11). Nebuchadnezzar became extremely angry and commanded all the wise men in Babylon be killed (Daniel 2:12).

**The deceitful wedding guests** – Jesus is teaching about the kingdom of heaven and spiritual matters, but I would like to break this parable down to the human elements. The king in the parable had prearranged with certain people to attend the wedding of his son (Matthew 22:2-4). When the time came for the event, all the guests declined to come (Matthew 22:5). Some even grew tired of the king's servants constant reminding and killed them (Matthew 22:6). The king became angry and sent his army to destroy them (Matthew 22:7). The king had a marriage feast ready and he was determined to have guests at the feast (Matthew 22:8). He instructed his servants to acquire guests where ever they could find them (Matthew 22:9.10). The king was angry at his 'friends'. He had told all of them that his son was going to be married and it followed that there would be a feast. They all knew when the day was and promised to come. The king was angry that his friends took the event and, by extension, him and his son so lightly. He was deceived by the people he considered his closest confidants.

## Loss of property –

The parable of the prodigal son not only teaches the unconditional love of a father and the forgiving nature of earthly fathers, and by extension our Heavenly Father, but it reveals something about the nature of the older brother who stayed behind. The younger brother had taken his inheritance and left the farm. Big brother then thought himself as an only heir to the remainder. No messages or news of his little brother caused him to consider him to be dead. So the elder went about his business of taking care of "his" property. Then one day, out of the blue, his brother came home! Their father not only had given him his portion previously, but now has thrown him a party and slaughtered the best calf on the place. Thus, giving him even more than his portion. The elder brother did not attend the 'welcome home party'. He was busy sulking because he was angry at the seemingly unfairness of the whole situation (Luke 15:11-32). Greed and self-assurances will always lull you into a false sense of security. "Neither give place to the devil." (Ephesians 4:27)

## Disobedience of the 'law' (Moses law) –

Many times the temple officials tried to catch Jesus in an offense so as to destroy or at least decrease His influence on the common man. Most of the accusations were about keeping the sabbath. The priests and rulers of the temple believed they were on solid ground with this accusation. It one of the ten commandments. "Remember the sabbath day, to keep it holy. Six days shalt thou labour, and do all thy work: But the seventh day is the sabbath of the LORD thy God: in it thou shalt not do any work, thou, nor thy son, nor thy daughter, thy manservant, nor thy maidservant, nor thy cattle, nor thy stranger that is within thy gates: For in six days the LORD made heaven and earth, the sea, and all that in them is, and rested the seventh day: wherefore the LORD blessed the sabbath day, and hallowed it." (Exodus 20:8-11) While they were attacking Jesus for working on the sabbath, they never considered that they were working on the sabbath. Both were doing God's work, therefore they should have been working together. The priests and rulers, however did not recognize that Jesus was the Son of God, only that He was messing up their good lifestyle and influence on the people. Jesus healed a woman that had "a spirit of infirmity for eighteen years" it had her bent over and she could not stand straight (Luke 13:1).

She glorified God for her healing and that made the rulers of the temple angry, the praise was supposed to come to the priests as representatives of God. When something good happened to one of the people they were supposed to bring a sacrifice to the temple, thereby enriching the priests. This woman just stood up straight and gave God the glory. We read, that through his indignation the ruler gave a mini-sermon. "And the ruler of the synagogue answered with indignation, because that Jesus had healed on the sabbath day, and said unto the people, There are six days in which men ought to work: in them therefore come and be healed, and not on the sabbath day." (Luke 13:14) He considered that healing was Jesus' job not the work of God. Jesus chided him by pointing out that each one takes his animals to be watered on the sabbath (Luke 13:15). Is an animal's comfort more important than a human's suffering (Luke 13:16). See also Luke 14:1-6; John 7:21-24

## God's return and rewarding of His people -

"And the nations were angry, and thy wrath is come, and the time of the dead, that they should be judged, and that thou shouldest give reward unto thy servants the prophets, and to the saints, and them that fear thy name, small and great; and shouldest destroy them which destroy the earth." (Revelation 11:18) There will be angry resentments in the world at the just appearance and action of the power of God, "The nations were angry..." (Revelation 11:18) Not only had the nations been angry, but will continue to be: their hearts will rise up against God; they will meet his wrath with their own anger. The nations are not ruled by those people whose face we see in the media. Those are the willing vessels. The nations are actually ruled by Satan. Remember, "For we wrestle not against flesh and blood, but against principalities, against powers, against the rulers of the darkness of this world, against spiritual wickedness in high places." (Ephesians 6:12) The evilness and corruption of this world is not from the minds and thoughts of the perpetrators. There is nothing new under the sun. The ruler of this world is Satan and he has not had a new idea since the beginning of time. Satan and his willing dupes will be extremely angry at this time because it will be the time when God, takes a just revenge upon the enemies of his people (us, the saints), repaying tribulation to those who had troubled them. It is the time in which he will begin to reward his people's faithful services and sufferings; and our enemies cannot bear it, they aggravate and provoke God spitefully and will increase their guilt and hastened their destruction.

## Fear of Holy retribution -

When the tribes of Reuben, Gad and half the tribe of Manasseh saw the land that they were lead into, they decided that it was a good place for their family, flocks and heard. They ask Moses to let them have the land east of the Jordan river for their inheritance. Moses agreed as long as the men would continue the journey and help the rest of the tribes fight and conquer their lands. The two and one half tribes agreed. (Numbers 32:1-33) When Israel had completely secured the land that God had lead them to and given to them for their possession. Joshua released the two and one half tribes to return to their families and their lands (Joshua 22:1-4). The men talked during the journey and were concerned that their heirs might be excluded from the opportunity to worship God with their brethren, since they were separated by the Jordan river (Joshua 22:10,24-28). The two and one half tribes came to the river Jordan and decided to build an alter like the one that God had instructed Moses to build as a witness to future generations that the people on that side of the river were the brethren of the people on the other side. The other tribes heard that they had built an altar and assumed that they had turned away from serving God and obeying His commandments (Joshua 22:16). The people had experienced God's wrath on the journey from Egypt and did not want to face that again (Joshua 22:17-20). They sent representatives to meet with the leaders of the two and one half tribes. The leaders of the two and one half tribes explained their motive for constructing the altar and the other tribes of Israel were satisfied (Joshua 22:30-33). God delivered the children of Israel from the cruelty of Egypt as one body of people and He wanted them to remain as one body so they would form a nation wholly dedicated to Him. "Ye have seen what I did unto the Egyptians, and how I bare you on eagles' wings, and brought you unto myself. Now therefore, if ye will obey my voice indeed, and keep my covenant, then ye shall be a peculiar treasure unto me above all people: for all the earth is mine: And ye shall be unto me a kingdom of priests, and an holy nation..." (Exodus 19:4-6)

## Disobedience to the law (man's law) –

Haman was a confidant to king Ahasuerus and a member of his court. He received a promotion to be head over all the king's courtiers (Esther 3:1). The king decreed that all subjects were to bow to Haman in honor of his position (Esther 3:2). Mordecai, the cousin and guardian of Esther the queen, and a Jew, refused to give homage to Haman (Esther 3:2-4). Haman became very angry with Mordecai because he would not bow to him as was decreed by the king, Ahasuerus (Esther 3:5). He was so angry that he determined to destroy all the Jews in the kingdom (Esther 3:6). He went to the king with a pretty affective but lame reason. "And Haman said unto king Ahasuerus, There is a certain people scattered abroad and dispersed among the people in all the provinces of thy kingdom; and their laws are diverse from all people; neither keep they the king's laws: therefore it is not for the king's profit to suffer them." (Esther 3:8) Haman convinced the king to make a law that any Jew found anywhere in the kingdom was to be killed. The Bible best describes the action and decree,

"And the letters were sent by posts into all the king's provinces, to destroy, to kill, and to cause to perish, all Jews, both young and old, little children and women, in one day, even upon the thirteenth day of the twelfth month, which is the month Adar, and to take the spoil of them for a prey." (Esther 3:13) Mordecai and the Jews mourned and put on sackcloth and ashes, fasted and prayed. Esther saw him and sent her attendant, Hathach, to ask the reason for his sorrow. Mordecai told the whole story to her Hathach and gave him a copy of the decree. Then Hathach reported back to Esther and told her the situation (Esther 4"1-9). The Jews were saved by Esther, the Jewess queen and Haman, who thought highly of himself was killed in the place he had prepared for the death of Mordecai. For a short time Haman's pride had created the beginning of a holocaust. God saved His chosen people by giving Ahasuerus insomnia and causing the king to desire to bestow honor upon Mordecai (Esther 6:1-3). Did he forget the decree he had signed for Haman to destroy all the Jews?

## Presumption of power –

Esther had prepared a banquet for the king and had him invite Haman. She did this two days in a row (Esther 5:1-8). The second day she revealed her request, to save her people, the Jews (Esther 7:1-4). Ahasuerus questioned her as to who it was that had set their heart on destroying the people (Esther 7:5). She told him that it was Haman (Esther 7:6). The news troubled the king because this situation set his queen and right hand man against one another (Esther 7:7). He left their presence to think over the solution to the situation. Haman seeing his future was bleak, fell on the couch (bed) of Esther to plead for his life (Esther 7:7). The king came back into the room at that time and assumed that Haman was trying to rape the queen (Esther 7:8). Talk about a case of bad timing! Ahasuerus was angry with Haman because he presumed he had the power to destroy the Jews under the protection of Ahasuerus. Then to make matters worse he attacked Esther. The king had him taken out and hung on the very gallows Haman had built to hang Mordecai (Esther 7:9,10). God will protect His people. "He suffered no man to do them wrong: yea, he reproved kings for their sakes; Saying, touch not mine anointed, and do my prophets no harm." (Psalms 105:14,15)

## Justifying yourself rather than justifying God –

The opening verse of the book of Job should be a description of all God fearing believers. "...that man was perfect and upright, and one that feared God, and eschewed evil." (Job 1:1) Eschewed means to shun or avoid. Job was considered a good, upright man who avoided evil at all costs. Satan sinned against God and was kicked out of his position in heaven but he is still under authority to God and there are still times when he is required to appear before God. When he does he condemns the righteous servants of God (Job 1:6; 2:1). God was proud of Job and allowed Satan to test him (Job 1:8-22; 2:3-7). God had allowed Satan to take all that Job had acquired and his son and daughters. He then returned to inflict him with painful boils from the bottom of his feet to the top of his head. Job took it all in stride and never cursed God or became angry (Job 1:20-22; 2:9,10). Three of Job's friends came to mourn with him. His condition was so severe that they hardly recognized him (Job 2:11-13). His friends kept trying to find out why all this had happened to a good God fearing man. Job continually argues that the misery came through no fault of his. He was innocent. The Bible says that Job was continually offering burnt offerings for himself and his children. "And it was so, when the days of their feasting were gone about, that Job sent and sanctified them, and rose up early in the morning, and offered burnt offerings according to the number of them all: for Job said, It may be that my sons have sinned, and cursed God in their hearts. Thus did Job continually." (Job 1:5) He did all the right things in the eyes and understanding of his friends, so why had God turned His back to Job. Job had to had sinned in some instance! Besides these three friends, one had brought a young man with him. This young man had sat and listened to his elders and finally had to speak himself (Job 32:2-7,9). He was angry that Job had maintained his innocence and had not acknowledged that God could have done this for little or no reason (Job 32:2). He points out that there is a spirit in all men. "But there is a spirit in man: and the inspiration of the Almighty giveth them understanding." (Job 32:8) Elihu asserts that God has done this to Job. "Yea, I attended unto you, and, behold, there was none of you that convinced Job, or that answered his words: Lest ye should say, We have found out wisdom: God thrusteth him down, not man." (Job 32:12,13) As we know, that he was closer to being right than the other three men. God did allow these afflictions to come upon Job through Satan. It came as a test, not as a punishment. This is an example of how Satan accuses the believers in an attempt to destroy us. "Be sober, be vigilant; because your adversary the devil, as a roaring lion, walketh about, seeking whom he may devour" (1 Peter 5:8) I like what Job's responses were to his losses and afflictions. The loss of his family and property brought a simple comment, the Lord gives and the Lord takes away. The boils brought his wife's disdain and her suggestion that he curse God and die. Job asked her that if we get good from the hand of God shouldn't we also accept loss and pain from God. How many of us can be that gracious in loss?

## Blasphemy –

**Jesus in the synagogue in His home city –** Jesus had received the baptism of the Holy Ghost, been to the dessert and defeated the devil's tempting and His time had come for Him to begin His ministry. Jesus went to the synagogue in His home city on the sabbath (Luke 4:16). He declared His Holy position to His family and friends (Luke 4:21). Those who heard Him in the synagogue knew Him as the son of Joseph, the carpenter, and did not understand that He was of a Holy patronage, 'The Son of God'. They thought that He was committing blasphemy, an offense worthy of death. The men in attendance at the synagogue were angry and ready to kill Jesus. They took Him to the edge of the cliff and were going to push Him off to punish Him for His crime (Luke 4:16-29). Those who know you the best will always be the hardest to convince of your calling and growth in Christ. "But Jesus said unto them, a prophet is not without honour, but in his own country, and among his own kin, and in his own house." (Mark 6:4) There was no way that this gentle man could be the Messiah that the Jews were waiting for!! According to Isaiah 61:2, the Christ would bring, "the acceptable year of the LORD, and the day of vengeance of our God". The Jews are expecting the Messiah to appear, be recognized and accepted by all then reap vengeance on all the unbelievers, non-Jews and their enemies. Thus freeing them of all their bondage and restoring their power and glory. This man, Jesus, was not going to do that! How could He proclaim Himself to be the Messiah?

**The stoning of Stephen -** Disciples of Jesus were multiplying, even a great number of priests were following the faith (Acts 6:7). Stephen was a man of honest report, full of the Holy Ghost and wisdom (Acts 6:3). "And Stephen, full of faith and power, did great wonders and miracles among the people." (Acts 6:8) He gained notice and popularity among the people. The leaders of the temple were against him for the same reasons they had been against Jesus and had Him crucified, he preached the gospel of grace. Stephen did not proclaim to be the Son of God, but he kept the way alive and convinced others that the Messiah had come and been killed by the temple leaders and raised on the third day. Stephen was very influential and was a threat to the priests sweet lifestyle. Stephen, therefore, must die!! The leadership was very angry with him. They hired unscrupulous men to lie and say that they had heard Stephen blaspheme (Acts 6:11-14). Didn't these same men hire unscrupulous men to lie against Jesus at His trial? On the testimony of the liars he was taken to the Sanhedrin for further questioning (Acts 6:12). Stephen laid out God's case against the nation of Israel, their continuous lack of obedience and trust in God (Acts 7:1-50). He concluded by affirming that Jesus was the Messiah that they had been waiting so long for. Their lack of belief and stiff-necked ways had killed Him as their fathers has killed the prophets sent before to foretell the coming 'of the Just One' (Acts 7:51-53). They were greatly angered at his words and they took him out and stoned him. Making Stephen the first martyr (Acts 7:54-60).

## Loss of job/wealth –

**Paul casts out the spirit of divination from the young woman** – One of Paul's missionary journeys took him into Philippi. While there a young lady that had a spirit of divination who followed Paul and his fellow travelers all around the city (Acts 16:16,17). She would cry out constantly, "These men are the servants of the most high God, which show unto us the way of salvation." (Acts 16:17) This disturbed Paul. The Scriptures say that he was 'grieved' and turned to the girl and cast out the spirit (Acts 16:17). As the story goes, this young woman was used by her masters to tell peoples fortunes, for a fee (Acts 16:16). Therefore, when they saw that her ability was gone and their hope for riches was destroyed, they became angry. They captured Paul and Silas and took them to the place where the leaders of the city held court (Acts 16:19). They did not accuse them of casting out demons or preaching the new way, Christianity. They knew that these accusations would not bring the revenge that they desired. The girl's masters accused them of subversion (Acts 16:20,21). Paul and Silas were stripped, beaten and thrown in jail (Acts 16:22-24).

**Demetrius, the silversmith, causes an uproar -** The third missionary journeys took Paul into Ephesus. There he met many who had heard about Jesus but their teachers were followers of John the Baptist or intellectual Jews who believed that Jesus was the Messiah and had no further knowledge (Acts 18:24-28; 19:1-7). When Paul explained the way more fully, he convinced many to turn from idols and false gods and worship and serve the true living God (Acts 19:8-10,26). Demetrius, the silversmith, made images of Diana for a living. Therefore, his and all the other idol makers business fell off sharply. Making Demetrius and his colleagues enraged. He called a meeting with his colleagues to put a stop to Paul's preaching that there is only one true God. The craftsmen filled the whole city with confusion and caught two of Paul's traveling companions and took them to the theater to put them on trial. Most of the people there were confused as to the charges against the men. The town clerk finally quieted the crowed and stated that if the craftsman had a problem with Paul and his travelers, let them take the matter before the leaders and the courts. This ended the uproar. There are still people who worship idols and false gods. Some do it unaware. Be careful who you choose to be taught by and how you follow God. You must pray, fast and read the Bible regularly to stay close to God and under His protection. Be very sure that you know the Word of God and can back up your arguments with Biblical truth. Even to those who have been in church for many years. If they are not Bible based they are wrong! The Bible has all the answers! Anything added or omitted will cause you to sin. "For I testify unto every man that heareth the words of the prophecy of this book, If any man shall add unto these things, God shall add unto him the plagues that are written in this book: And if any man shall take away from the words of the book of this prophecy, God shall take away his part out of the book of life, and out of the holy city, and from the things which are written in this book." (Revelation 22:18,19) This means the whole Bible, not just the Book of Revelation.

## Being rushed to accomplish a purpose -

Although, not a human Satan is a Bible character and does get angry. He is constantly angry, he lost his position and home in heaven and then Jesus defeated him and now has the keys to hell and rules the earth. All the old devil can do is roam the earth like a vagabond looking for trouble and creating it if he cannot find it. Then he runs to God and accuses men and mankind of the sins he, himself caused. Satan was the most favored angel until pride overcame him and he was cast out of heaven (Revelation 12:7-9). His time is short upon the earth and he knows it. He will torment the earth dwellers to get revenge for events that happened in heaven (Revelation 12:10-12). He now roams the earth and is the ruler of the disobedient, that is the unbeliever. "Be sober, be vigilant; because your adversary the devil, as a roaring lion, walketh about, seeking whom he may devour..." (1 Peter 5:8) "Wherein in time past ye walked according to the course of this world, according to the prince of the power of the air, the spirit that now worketh in the children of disobedience..." (Ephesians 2:2) Satan was demoted from being the head angel to being totally kicked out of heaven (Revelation 12:8). We know that the devil is always angry. He tried to destroy Jesus before His ministry began by tempting Him in the wilderness (Matthew 4:1-11, Luke 4:1-13). Revelation 12:1,2;5,6 tell us that a woman of greatness, Israel, gave birth to an male child that is to rule the earth. The dragon, Satan, tried to catch the child to destroy Him and also destroy the woman. The child was caught up to heaven and the woman was taken to a safe place. This enraged the old devil so much that he tried to destroy her by drowning her with a flood of water from his mouth (Revelation 12:15). The earth opened up and the water was taken into the deep and wide opening, saving the woman (Revelation 12:16). Do we need to mention how mad this made Satan. He could no longer get to the woman or her child, so he came after the children of God. "And the dragon was wroth with the woman, and went to make war with the remnant of her seed, which keep the commandments of God, and have the testimony of Jesus Christ." (Revelation 12:17) This is where we, as believers and followers of Christ, enter the battle. We " have the testimony of Jesus Christ" and therefore are an enemy of the devil's. "For we wrestle not against flesh and blood, but against principalities, against powers, against the rulers of the darkness of this world, against spiritual wickedness in high places." (Ephesians 6:12) It should be no surprise to find that Satan is angry. He is always angry!! How would you like to be kicked out of paradise? Then have just a short time to seek your revenge. Your end will be a bottomless pit. This is Satan's destiny. Praise God!!

## Suffering an insult –

Namaan the leprous captain of the army of Syria went all the way to Samaria to be healed on the word of a young maid (2 Kings 5:1-5). This was discussed earlier in another context. We will examine the story here from the point of view of Namaan. After he had traveled all that way to see Elisha, the prophet never came out to see him. As further insult, he sent a messenger to give him some lame instructions about going for a swim. If that was all he had to do, he could have stayed in Syria and had cleaner water to jump into (2 Kings 5:8-12). Namaan was insulted. He was a man in charge of many men and this man that was supposed to heal him never even came to his door to wave at him. The inhospitable way he was treated enraged him so much that he gave up on being healed and was going to return to his house.

His servants talked him into following the prophets instructions (2 Kings 5:13). Guess what?!? Did you remember from earlier? Namaan was healed when he dipped himself in the Jordan river! (2 Kings 5:14) It should come as no surprise, good things will come our way if we obey God. Even if what He asks us to do seems silly or foolhardy.

## Being told your faults or mistakes -

**Hanani rebukes Asa -** Israel was a divided country for many years. One section was called Judah and the other section was known as Israel. They were always warring against each other. On one of those occasions Baasha, the king of Israel decided to build a city to block trade to Judah effectively laying siege to the city without directly attacking the main cities and tying up troops (2 Chronicles 16:1). When Asa, king of Judah, saw and realized his fate he sent messengers to Ben-hadad, king of Syria to help him. He sent gold and silver from the palace and from the temple to buy his services (2 Chronicles 16:2). While this allegiance was successful in that Ben-hadad attacked the cities of Israel and made Baasha stop building and return to his country to protect his people (2 Chronicles 16:4,5). It was expensive in that it cleaned out the treasuries of the country and the house of God (2 Chronicles 16:2). There was a cheaper alternative! Hanani, a prophet, approached Asa and rebuked him for not calling on the LORD (2 Chronicles 16:7). He reminded the king of a time when he had relied on the LORD and was victorious (2 Chronicles 16:8). I love the words Hanani uses to rebuke Asa. "For the eyes of the LORD run to and fro throughout the whole earth, to show himself strong in the behalf of them whose heart is perfect toward him. Herein thou hast done foolishly: therefore from henceforth thou shalt have wars." (2 Chronicles 16:9) If Asa had of turned to God for help, he would have been victorious and not had to lose the gold or silver. Here is a promise that we can all grab onto. If our hearts are right with God he will show His strength in our behalf and protect us from our enemies. Our job... to keep our hearts perfect toward Him.

**Uzziah attempts to offer incense in the temple** - Uzziah was made king of Judah at the age of sixteen (2 Chronicles 26:1,3). He was a God fearing man (2 Chronicles 26:4,5). He reigned for fifty two years and God made him victorious in many battles. He had many fields of crops and many head of livestock. He fortified Judah and supplied the army with the equipment they needed. (2 Chronicles 26:6-15) The citizens appreciated all that he did for them. Pride entered into Uzziah. He decided that he was going to offer incense to the LORD himself. This was the priest's job and Mosaic law forbid anyone other than a priest to work in the temple. The High Priest and eighty priests tried to stop him and he became very angry and resisted them and physically fought against them. He was so determined to burn his incense (2 Chronicles 26:16-19). Uzziah did not listen to the priests so God took part in the situation. He struck Uzziah with leprosy. The priests watched the condition come over him right in front of their eyes (2 Chronicles 26:19,20). The fight was over at that point. Uzziah, himself fled from the temple. He forgot all about burning the incense! (2 Chronicles 26:19,20) It should be noted that God did not kill Uzziah but separated him from the people and his duties as king. He was a leper until the day he died (2 Chronicles 26:21). He was considered unclean and could have no contact with other people. His son, Jotham, had to rule in his place (2 Chronicles 26:21). This story is a great example of how a believer can start so powerfully right with God, get comfortable and full of himself or herself, then lose all in the end. Let's review a couple of scriptures. Uzziah started his kingship on the right path, "And he did that which was right in the sight of the LORD, according to all that his father Amaziah did. And he sought God in the days of Zechariah, who had understanding in the visions of God: and as long as he sought the LORD, God made him to prosper." (2 Chronicles 26:4,5) The end of his reign is marred with a transgression against the LORD. "But when he was strong, his heart was lifted up to his destruction: for he transgressed against the LORD his God, and went into the temple of the LORD to burn incense upon the altar of incense." (2 Chronicles 26:16)

## Someone taking advantage of a relative –

**The defilement of Dinah** – Dinah, the only known daughter of Jacob, was most likely kept pretty close to the tents of her father. Jacob had moved his family often since he left the home of Laban. Dinah, being the only girl and therefore having no other companions was naturally inquisitive about the local girls. It is assumed that she was about fifteen or sixteen at this time. She ventured out from her father's home and into the nearby town of Shalem (Genesis 33:18, 34:1). She caught the eye of Shechem, the prince of the region. Probably considered the most desired bachelor. He seduced her and defiled her (Genesis 34:2). When the deed was known, Jacob and her brothers were enraged (Genesis 34:5,7). Shechem's father Hamor went to Jacob to try to arrange a marriage between Shechem and Dinah (Genesis 34:6,8-10). Shechem loved Dinah very much (Genesis 34:3,11,12). The anger of Jacob and his sons toward Shechem is easy to understand. While the deed was not labeled as 'rape', Dinah was certainly taken advantage of by an older more experienced man. He undoubtedly was very desirable to the local maidens.

**Amnon defiles Tamar** – Amnon, one of David's sons, loved Tamar, one of David's daughters. She was the sister of Absalom. Absalom and Tamar were from a different mother than Amnon. Amnon loved Tamar so much and he pined for her to the point that it made him physically sick (2 Samuel 13:1,2). He and a friend of his came up with a scheme to bring her to him with the kings permission (2 Samuel 13:3-6). Amnon would pretend to be severely ill and he would request that Tamar would act as his nurse and tend to him. The ruse worked and David sent for Tamar to attend to Amnon (2 Samuel 13:7-10). Once she was in his chamber (bedroom) alone with him, he tried to seduce her (2 Samuel 13:11-13). When she refused his advances he took her by force (2 Samuel 13:14). Once the deed was done he hated her and had her thrown out seeing he had no more use for her (2 Samuel 13:15-17). Tamar had worn a robe of many colors, as was her right as a virgin daughter of the king (2 Samuel 13:18). Being no longer qualified to wear the robe, she tore it and covered her head with ashes as a symbol of mourning (2 Samuel 13:19). Her brother Absalom saw her ask about her grief and she told him the whole sordid tale (2 Samuel 13:20). King David became enraged, Absalom held his peace but hated Amnon thereafter (2 Samuel 13:21,22). They say that revenge is a dish best serve cold. Absalom waited two whole years! He threw a feast at sheep shearing time and invited all the king's sons (2 Samuel 13:23-27). He had arranged for his servants to kill Amnon when he was relaxed, unsuspecting and drunk (2 Samuel 13:28,29). Thus did Absalom avenge his sister's honor. Sin will always tear a family apart. David lost a son and Tamar never married. She never gave David grandchildren (2 Samuel 13:20). That was two branches of the family tree that never developed.

## Unspecified offense –

There are three instances when anger surfaces and there are no specific details or reasons given. Pharaoh was angry at his butler and baker and had them imprisoned (Genesis 40:1,2). His anger and the punishment of imprisonment did however, serve to acquaint them with Joseph and secure his release (Genesis 41:10).

In Esther two of Ahasuerus's guards were angry to the point of conspiring to do the king harm (Esther 2:21). Again there are no details as to why these guards were angry at the king. The book of Acts tells us that Herod was displeased with Tyre and Sidon, two cities on the coast in the land of the Phoenician's, to the point he thought to attack them (Acts 12:20).

## Treason –

David was anointed king of Israel by Samuel (1 Samuel 16:1,11-13). Saul was still alive and sat on the throne but in God's eyes, David was the king. God's spirit left Saul (1 Samuel 16:14) and went to David (1 Samuel 16:13). David respected the kingdom rule and never challenged Saul for the throne, even though it was his rightful position. Saul was troubled by an evil spirit from God (1 Samuel 16:14). He perceived that David was a threat to his kingship and his families dynasty (1 Samuel 18:8,9;20:31). Saul tried to kill David many times, but David never fought back. That would have caused a civil war and divided the kingdom. Instead he ran and hid himself and avoided Saul at all cost. David hid out in the land of the Philistine's (1 Samuel 27:1-4). The Philistines and Israel were always at war. On one of these occasions, David and his men went to fight with Israel on the side of the Philistines. The princes of the Philistines did not trust David to remain loyal. They believed that David would use the opportunity to get back into Saul's good graces by attacking them in the heat of battle (1 Samuel 29:1-7). The princes complained to their king and to make sure that the focus was on the Israeli army and the princes were not watching their backs for David's surprise attack, he sent David and his men home. The leaders of the army of the Philistines were so mistrustful of David that they became angry when they were going to have to fight alongside of him. Does anyone remember Goliath? They did!!

## Weak faith of a friend God wishes to bless –

Elisha was sick and dying but still carried on his duties as a prophet of God (2 Kings 13:14). Israel and Syria were in and out of wars with each other. Joash, the king of Israel, Came to visit him and ask for God's instructions for the upcoming battle (2 Kings 13:14). One of Elisha's last acts was to prophesy of Israel's conquests (2 Kings 13:15-17). He called the arrows, "The arrow of the LORD'S deliverance, and the arrow of deliverance from Syria..." (2 Kings 13:17) He had Joash shoot the arrows toward Syria in the east. Elisha instructed Joash, the king of Israel to take the arrows and strike the ground. Joash struck the ground three times and stopped (2 Kings 13:18). The prophet became enraged with the kings action. Remember these arrows are the "The arrow of the LORD'S deliverance, and the arrow of deliverance from Syria." They were endued with power from God. Stopping at three showed a lack of faith in God's delivering power. Elisha points out to him that he should have had trust in God and struck the ground five or six times (2 Kings 13:19). We deny ourselves blessings or power that God wants to bestow upon us by selling ourselves short and obeying just for a little while. Stopping short when we get tired of life gets in the way. It is easy to walk to a neighbor's house a short distance away. A journey of many miles is more difficult and easier not even start. "I returned, and saw under the sun, that the race is not to the swift, nor the battle to the strong, neither yet bread to the wise, nor yet riches to men of understanding, nor yet favour to men of skill; but time and chance happeneth to them all." (Ecclesiastes 9:11)

## Restoration of Jerusalem –

The Jews were in captivity in Persia. Nehemiah, one of the captured Jews, had risen to the rank of 'cupbearer' to Artaxerxes, the king (Nehemiah 1:1). He had heard about the conditions in Jerusalem and of those who remained behind (Nehemiah

1:2,3). Being a Jew, he was tenderhearted for the city and the people (Nehemiah 1:4). He ask Artaxerxes for permission to visit Jerusalem and rebuild the city walls (Nehemiah 2:1-6). The king gave his permission and letters of authority to Nehemiah (Nehemiah 2:7-9). There were Samaritan occupying armies stationed in and around Jerusalem. One of the captain's names was Sanballat and his servant with him was Tobiah and they were not very happy with the fact that someone had come, with permission of the king, to rebuild the walls of Jerusalem (Nehemiah 2:10). Sanballat became enraged when the wall actually started to be built and ridiculed the workers and the work (Nehemiah 4:1-3). When the work did not stop, Sanballat conspired with other enemies of Judah to attack the workers and stop the progress permanently (Nehemiah 4:7,8). When we do God's work somebody is going to get angry. Satan is always lurking around where God's work is being performed trying to hinder or stop it totally.

## Perceived treason –

The Chaldeans had surrounded Jerusalem and Zedekiah, the king of the city, sent for help from Egypt (Jeremiah 37:5). God was not with the Jews in this battle. He had sent the Chaldeans to punish them because they did not honor God. "But neither he, nor his servants, nor the people of the land, did hearken unto the words of the LORD, which he spake by the prophet Jeremiah." (Jeremiah 37:2) Jeremiah prophesied against Jerusalem. "Then came the word of the LORD unto the prophet Jeremiah, saying, Thus saith the LORD, the God of Israel; Thus shall ye say to the king of Judah, that sent you unto me to inquire of me; Behold, Pharaoh's army, which is come forth to help you, shall return to Egypt into their own land. And the Chaldeans shall come again, and fight against this city, and take it, and burn it with fire. Thus saith the LORD; Deceive not yourselves, saying, The Chaldeans shall surely depart from us: for they shall not depart. For though ye had smitten the whole army of the Chaldeans that fight against you, and there remained but wounded men among them, yet should they rise up every man in his tent, and burn this city with fire." (Jeremiah 37:6-10) When the Chaldeans heard that the Egyptians were on their way, they withdrew from Jerusalem (Jeremiah 37:11). Since Jeremiah had prophesied for the enemy against Jerusalem the leaders assumed that Jeremiah had conspired with the Chaldeans. Thereby committing treason. Jeremiah was leaving the city to escape the coming war when he was captured and taken to the princes of the land (Jeremiah 37:12-14). The princes were convinced that he was guilty, especially since he was leaving Jerusalem, they became very angry and beat him and had him imprisoned (Jeremiah 37:15). The ways of God are not understood by the unbelievers which is why we must avoid the very appearance of impropriety. "Abstain from all appearance of evil." (1Thessalonians 5:22)

## Being mocked –

We all know the story of Jesus' birth and the visitation of the wise men. The angle I want to discuss here is Herod's duplicity and cruelty. Herod was a descendant of Esau. The land he occupied was brought into Jewish control about 130A.D. This meant that those inhabitants could be considered Jews if they were circumcised and obeyed the Jewish laws. The natural born Jews, however, considered them 'half-Jew' and basically outsiders. When the Jewish nation was conquered by the Romans there was no greater insult to the Jews than to make a 'half-Jew' their governor. The distrust between these two peoples created a perfect situation whereby Rome could rule the area and have a Jew in direct power. Actually Herod's power was very limited. He ruled only as long as the Romans were satisfied with his performance. The birth of another 'king' would be bad news for him. Wise men from the east were going throughout his territory asking for the location of this baby king (Matthew 2:1,2). The news that there was a babe considered "The King of The Jews" then was a terrible threat to his position (Matthew 2:3). The Emperor of Rome was supposed to be considered as the king of the region. The country was occupied by Rome and therefore was a territory of Rome and under Roman rule. Herod was just a local figurehead. Herod called the wise men to him and made a pact with them to find the location of the child and to let him know so he could go and worship Him, too (Matthew 2:7,8). He had no intention to seek out and worship the Christ Child. He only wanted them to do his footwork and find the babe. The wise men never returned to him as agreed (Matthew 2:12). Herod was enraged! His solution was to kill all the babies of Bethlehem the approximate age of Jesus (Matthew 2:16). We all knew that what Herod had in mind all along was to kill Jesus and stop the 'king of the Jew' nonsense being spread about by the people. Praise the LORD!! God had other plans.

## Ingratitude –

Jesus taught with the parable of the 'wicked servant' about spiritual matters. Let's look at this from a human perspective. In this parable, a servant owed his lord ten thousand talents which he could not pay (Matthew 18:24,25). His master declared severe measures whereby he might recover some of his money (Matthew 18:25). The servant begged him for mercy and his debtor had compassion for him and the master canceled the whole debt (Matthew 18:26,27). That same debtor then went out and found a fellow who owed him one hundred pence (Matthew 18:28). When he could not pay, the fellow servant ask him for mercy, using the same words he had just used to his master (Matthew 18:29). He did not give mercy as he had just received it, instead he dealt harshly with the one who owed him (Matthew 18:30). The lord was angry because in receiving a kindness, the debtor should have given a kindness (Matthew 18:32-34). The master's servant was grateful that his debts were gone but that gratitude did not carry any further that his own pockets. Because he was a selfish man, his master reinstituted his debt and turned him over to people who would collect it. Jesus says it best, "So likewise shall my heavenly Father do also unto you, if ye from your hearts forgive not everyone his brother their trespasses." (Matthew 18:35) Thanks to Jesus' sacrifice you can mark all those sin and trespass debts, "PAID IN FULL!" How can you repay God for all He has done for us? He doesn't take MasterCard!! You have to forgive those who have done and still do you wrong. Jesus tells us how to repay Him and thank Him. "This is my commandment, That ye love one another, as I have loved you." (John 15:12) To honor God we must 'love one another'.

## Switched blessings –

The custom was to give the best blessing to the oldest child. When Israel blessed the children of Joseph he purposely crossed his hands thereby by switching the order of the blessings (Genesis 48:13,14). Joseph, was displeased at the location of his father's hands. He assumed that his father was confused because of his failing eye-sight and tried to straighten out the error (Genesis 48:17,18). Israel knew what he was doing and told Joseph that he knew (Genesis 48:19). He claimed them as his children and blessed them that day as God directed him (Genesis 48:16). "And he blessed them that day, saying, In thee shall Israel bless, saying, God make thee as Ephraim and as Manasseh: and he set Ephraim before Manasseh." (Genesis 48:20) Joseph's mistake was in associating God's grace to the order of nature. Manasseh was the oldest Joseph assumed that the blessing would fall in order of age. Nature is the creation and God is the creator. It is easy to become confused if we do not listen to God, our creator.

## Forsaking God in favor of man (a king) –

The people of Israel had inhabited their inheritance for a while and observed the kingdoms around them. They saw that the main difference between themselves and their neighbors was that their neighbors could see their sovereign ruler and the Israelites did not have a certain person they could point to as being in charge. The only evidence of their King, God, was His Shekinah Glory. Also, Samuel was getting old and had turned the duties of the judging of the nation over to his two sons (1 Samuel 8:1,2). They were not as upright and honest as Samuel was. The Bible says, "And his sons walked not in his ways, but turned aside after lucre, and took bribes, and perverted judgment." (1 Samuel 8:3) Lucre means money. Where you have this kind of justice, you actually have no justice! The elders formed a committee and went to Samuel's house and related the situation to him and ask him to appoint a king over them (1 Samuel 8:4,5). This was their solution to the corruption of Samuel's sons. Samuel was displeased when the people wanted to be ruled by a man in lieu of God (1 Samuel 8:6). Samuel prayed and God's answer was to let them have their king. I can't state God's answer as well as He did so here it is directly from the scriptures, "And the LORD said unto Samuel, Hearken unto the voice of the people in all that they say unto thee: for they have not rejected thee, but they have rejected me, that I should not reign over them. According to all the works which they have done since the day that I brought them up out of Egypt even unto this day, wherewith they have forsaken me, and served other gods, so do they also unto thee. Now therefore hearken unto their voice: howbeit yet protest solemnly unto them, and show them the manner of the king that shall reign over them." (1 Samuel 8:7-9) The warning and situations created by having a king listed in verses 10-18 were not heeded and Israel got their desire (1 Samuel 8:19-22). If you are serving God and He is truly your King... do not covet what those around you have. The grass is **never** greener!

## Unjust judgment (seemingly) –

David was displeased because God had slain Uzzah. We dealt with this story in the chapter dealing with God's anger. Here we will look at the text from the human prospective. David had taken council with his advisers and determined to relocate the ark of God to the city of Jerusalem (1 Chronicles 13:1-4). A great multitude gathered to go retrieve the ark (1 Chronicles 13:5,6). We discussed the fact earlier that according to the law the ark was to be carried by the poles associated with the ark on the shoulders of the Kohathites who were assigned this responsibility (Numbers 7:9). There was no cart to be used, new or old. I have to wonder how they loaded the ark on the cart. If they had touched it those who bore the burden would have been killed then. They had to use the poles to load it and those who loaded it had to be Kohathites. Otherwise, they would have been killed loading the ark on the cart. Also, why didn't David or one of his priests research out the proper method of transporting the ark? Never the less, the project was under taken and the ark was put on the cart (1 Chronicles 13:7). The people were extremely joyful and celebrated with singing, playing on musical instruments and dancing (1 Chronicles 13:8). During the journey the ground became uneven and the oxen stumbled threatening to turn the cart over, Uzzah reached out and touched the ark to steady and secure it (1 Chronicles 13:9). God struck him dead immediately!! David saw this as the end of his mission (1 Chronicles 13:11,12). "And David was afraid of God that day, saying, How shall I bring the ark of God home to me?" (1 Chronicles 13:12) Being fearful and not willing to continue the journey, David had the ark stored in the house of Obed-edom (1 Chronicles 13:13). The ark stayed with Obed-edom three months (1 Chronicles 13:14).

David had such high expectations about the relocation of the ark. He had planned a parade from its resting place all the way to Jerusalem. When Uzzah was killed, the party was over, the crowd dispersed and the merriment was gone. As happy as David was, he was stymied as to how to retrieve the ark. The Bible says that David was disappointed, I believe that he was stunned and angry at the situation. He could not get angry at God. Imagine the consequences of that!! This is a reminder of the spiritual truth that blessings does not follow even the best intentions in the service of God. He prescribes a method for accomplishing His work and any deviation from God's way will bring disaster.

## Judgment received from God –

Ben-hadad, the king of Syria, desired to conquer Samaria. He gathered his army and surrounded the city (1 Kings 20:1). Looking to start a war, he made ridiculous demands (1 Kings 20:2,3,5,6). Ahab, the king of Samaria, said he would submit at first, then after he met with the elders and all the people, he sent a message to Ben-hadad telling him not to be over confident (1 Kings 20:4,7-9,11). Ben-hadad had his war (1 Kings 20:12). While the armies of Syria were getting into position, God sent a prophet to Ahab and promised to give him the victory (1 Kings 20:1). Samaria routed Syria! God will always keep His word. Ben-hadad escaped and went home to Syria (1 Kings 20:20,21). God warned Ahab that Ben-hadad would return and to get prepared (1 Kings 20:22). God had marked Ben-hadad for destruction (1 Kings 20:42). Therefore, He had the advisers of Syria reason that they were defeated because "their gods are the gods of the hills" and they could be beaten if the battle took place on the plains (1 Kings 20:23). Ben-hadad fielded an army as large as the one that was destroyed in the first campaign (1 Kings 20:25). The promise of God differed slightly in this second campaign. Let's compare the two prophesies: "And, behold, there came a prophet unto

Ahab king of Israel, saying, Thus saith the LORD, Hast thou seen all this great multitude? behold, I will deliver it into thine hand this day; and thou shalt know that I am the LORD." (1 Kings 20:13) and the second is, "And there came a man of God, and spake unto the king of Israel, and said, Thus saith the LORD, Because the Syrians have said, The LORD is God of the hills, but he is not God of the valleys, therefore will I deliver all this great multitude into thine hand, and ye shall know that I am the LORD." (1 Kings 20:28) They are very similar, note that in the first God says He will deliver the 'multitude' into Ahab's hand and the second promise is that He would, "deliver all this great multitude into thine hand." The word 'all' indicating that every person was to be destroyed. Once again, Ben-hadad managed to escape death on the battlefield. He ran and cowered in an inner room in the city (1 Kings 20:30). His own men convinced him to beg for mercy from the princes of Samaria (1 Kings 20:31-33). Ahab made a covenant with him and let him go (1 Kings 20:34). God had marked Ben-hadad for destruction. Ahab had thwarted God's plan so the life of Ahab was required in exchange for the covenant he made with Ben-hadad (1 Kings 20:38-42). Judgment being passed on Ahab by God made him disheartened and naturally displeased (1 Kings 20:43). He could have ask for forgiveness and an opportunity to correct the situation. Sadly, no, he just slunk away home to await his fate.

## Jesus receiving praise from the people –

Jesus was in the temple healing the blind and the lame (Matthew 21:14). There was celebrating all around because of the healing work of Jesus (Matthew 21:15). The chief priests and scribes did not like Him healing on the sabbath and here He was healing in the temple, their territory. To make matters worse the people were praising Him, thereby ascribing Godly characteristics to Him (Matthew 21:15). The chief priests ask Him if He heard that the people were praising Him as God. Jesus replied that He heard and there was no problem because the unlearned are more intuitive to spiritual matters. The actual verse is, "And said unto him, Hearest thou what these say? And Jesus saith unto them, Yea; have ye never read, Out of the mouth of babes and sucklings thou hast perfected praise?" (Matthew 21:16) The priests and scribes should have been the first to recognized the Messiah. They were more worried that He was trying to take their positions or destroy the Jewish religion by doing away with the Mosaic laws and traditions. He drew a larger crowd of 'willing' followers than the priests and scribes did. Most of those who came to hear them had to because it was required by law. They were very displeased with most things that Jesus did and all that He gained.

## Stopping the children from seeing Jesus –

We all know that Jesus is not a normal human, even here on earth He was God. I have included this story here because He was, at the time, considered to be a human teacher or prophet by the people. The followers of Jesus brought their children to Him to be touched and blessed (Mark 10:13). The disciples rebuked the parents but Jesus heard them and was very much displeased (Mark 10:14). The literal translation from the Greek is 'moved with indignation.' Jesus experienced everything in His human form as we do. Here we have him experiencing indignation with His disciples. He came to earth to make all of us the children of God regardless of age. "Suffer the little children to come unto me, and forbid them not: for of such is the kingdom of God. Verily I say unto you, Whosoever shall not receive the kingdom of God as a little child, he shall not enter therein." (Mark 10:14,15) The children were allowed to go to Jesus and He did a very fatherly thing. "And he took them up in his arms, put his hands upon them, and blessed them." (Mark 10:16) Whether we are newborn or one hundred years old we are all God's children.

## Self-Importance -

There were two of Jesus' disciples that desired to sit next to Jesus in heaven (Matt.20:20; Mark 10:37). The right and left hand of God are places of honor and reserved for whomever God so desires to put there (Matt.20:23; Mark 10:40). James and John, the sons of Zebedee, thought of themselves so highly that they desired to be at the top spots in heaven and ask Jesus to grant it to them (Matt.20:20,21; Mark 10:35-37). When the other ten disciples heard of the request they were moved with indignation (Matt.20:24; Mark 10:41). Jesus used this as a teaching opportunity. He explained that service is the greatest position in the kingdom not lordship. "...but whosoever will be great among you, let him be your minister; And whosoever will be chief among you, let him be your servant: Even as the Son of man came not to be ministered unto, but to minister, and to give his life a ransom for many." (Matthew 20:26-28)

## Sacrificing to Molech (or any other false god) -

When Ahab, the king of Israel, was alive, the Moabites were subject to Israel and paid tribute to the king (2 Kings 3:4). When Ahab died, Mesha, the king of Moab decided that it was time to be free of Israel's control (2 Kings 3:5). The kings of Israel, Judah and Edom gathered themselves to go into battle against Moab (2 Kings 3:6-9). The king of Israel was not a true follower of God (2 Kings 3:1-3). He doubted that the battle would be won by them. "And the king of Israel said, Alas! that the LORD hath called these three kings together, to deliver them into the hand of Moab!" (2 Kings 3:10) The king of Judah, Jehoshaphat, called for a prophet of God to advise them (2 Kings 3:11). God told them through the prophet, Elisha, how to get water for their horses, cattle and themselves and at the same time defeat the Moabites (2 Kings 3:16-18). They were told to dig ditches all through the valley. The ditches filled up with water from God. At sunrise the water reflected the morning sun and shown as a sea of red. The Moabite knew that there was no water there only dirt, so when they saw the sea of red they assumed that the opposing armies had killed each other during the night. They rushed down to collect the spoils, only to be met by a fully trained and equipped army. Thus they were routed and chased back to their country and into their city (2 Kings 3:20-24). The king of Moab realized that the battle was lost to him, he made a sacrifice to his god to gain favor and turn the tide of the battle. His god was Molech. Molech demanded that those who served him would sacrifice their firstborn child to him by making them walk through fire. The children, of course, would die. Being under subjection to Israel, the Moabites should have been sacrificing to and worshiping the one true God of Israel. Which would include following the ten commandments. They obviously held to their old traditions, which is why God put them under the control of Israel to begin with and then delivered them into the hands of the coalition of the three kings. The king of Moab sacrificed his son (the next in line to the throne) to Molech. The Moabites had great indignation for Israel because their royal line of succession was now broken. Israel withdrew from the battle because the sacrificing to any other god was an abomination to them (2 Kings 3:26,27). "Thou shalt have no other gods before me. Thou shalt not make unto thee any graven image, or any likeness of anything that is in heaven above, or that is in the earth beneath, or that is in the water under the earth: Thou shalt not bow down thyself to them, nor serve them: for I the LORD thy God am a jealous God, visiting the iniquity of the fathers upon the children unto the third and fourth generation of them that hate me..." (Exodus 20:3-5)

## Wasting money –

Jesus was at Bethany, six days before Passover, at the house of Simon the leper (Matthew 26:6; Mark 14:3; John 12:1). While

He sat eating, Mary, the sister of Lazarus came in and poured spikenard on Him (Matthew 26:7; Mark 14:3; John 12:3). This ointment was very costly because it came from East India. The disciples, especially Judas Iscariot, considered the use of this ointment in this manner a waste. They only considered its value in monetary worth (Matthew 26:8,9; Mark 14:4,5; John 12:4-6). Mary was the only one who had taken Jesus serious when He talked about His death and had procured a burial spice for Him. Jesus perceived that Mary had understood His message and prepared Him for His upcoming ordeal the best she could. He chastised His disciples indignation and lack of understanding of coming events (Matthew 26:10-12; Mark 14:6-8; John 12:7,8). Mark records it best, "And Jesus said, Let her alone; why trouble ye her? she hath wrought a good work on me. For ye have the poor with you always, and whensoever ye will ye may do them good: but me ye have not always. She hath done what she could: she is come aforehand to anoint my body to the burying." (Mark 14:6-8) Money is not important to God! Jesus read Mary's heart while the disciples saw only the cash value of the product. I find it interesting that Judas, the disciple in charge of the purse, knew exactly what the spice was worth (John 12:4,5).

## Loss of status or position –

The people were gathered in the temple with the apostles and they performed many signs and wonders and miracles (Acts 5:12). The power of the Holy Spirit was so strong that just Peter's shadow falling on the sick would heal them (Acts 5:15). Many believed and were added to the LORD (Acts 5:14). The high priest and Sadducees were watching and observed these mighty events. When they had seen enough to arouse their indignation, they arrested the apostles and had them thrown into prison (Acts 5:17,18). The Sadducees were a sect of the Jews that denied the existence of angels or other spirits, and all miracles, especially the resurrection of the body. They were the religious rationalists of the time, and were strongly entrenched in the Sanhedrin and priesthood. The Sadducees are identified with no affirmative doctrine, but were mere deniers of the supernatural, they witnessed the great miracles that the apostles did with their own eyes and still denied the coming of the Messiah. The more people that believed in Christ and joined the new way the less came to temple on the Sabbath. Of course this aggravated the priests and temple leadership. God's church was growing and Satan's influence was diminishing. The more that the Church increases, the more the rage of Satan increases. Therefore the actions of the followers of the devil, although they didn't realize they were, proceeded from threatening to the imprisonment of the apostles (Acts 5:17,18).

## The arrest of Jesus –

We protect what is dear and precious to us. Jesus had just ate the Passover with His disciples (Luke 22:7-16). He had told them of all the things to come during that time. He told them of the coming conflict. "And he said unto them, When I sent you without purse, and scrip, and shoes, lacked ye anything? And they said, Nothing. Then said he unto them, but now, he that hath a purse, let him take it, and likewise his scrip: and he that hath no sword, let him sell his garment, and buy one. For I say unto you, that this that is written must yet be accomplished in me, And he was reckoned among the transgressors: for the things concerning me have an end. And they said, Lord, behold, here are two swords. And he said unto them, It is enough." (Luke 22:35-38) The disciples were thinking of earthly warfare but Jesus was speaking of spiritual warfare. He says all this using an allegory, as if he said, "O my friends and fellow soldiers, you have lived until now in relative peace: but now there is at hand a most severe battle to be fought, and you must therefore lay all other things aside and think about dressing yourselves in armor."

And what this armor is, is shown by his own example, when he prayed afterward in the garden and reproved Peter for striking with the sword. A great multitude came out to arrest Him, led by Judas Iscariot. Jesus said that they didn't need all those people to arrest Him. He was with them daily, peacefully among them; they could have taken Him at any time. He said, "... but this is your hour, and the power of darkness." (Luke 22:53) Satan was in control of this situation and he was to win this skirmish. Jesus went to the garden of Gethsemane to pray with Peter, James and John (Mark 14:32-34). Judas knew where Jesus would have gone. He lead those who were to arrest Jesus to Him (John 18:2,3). Peter, being of an earthly mindset, had brought a sword. When the men came near to arrest Jesus, he sprang into action to protect his master and cut off one of the high priest's servant's ears (John 18:10). Peter was determined to save his friend and teacher from anything that would take Him from them. We should keep in mind that we can do the wrong thing for the right reasons if we are not in the will of God. We must be aware that God has His ways and sometimes they are not obvious to us. For a deeper understanding see also: Matthew 26:47-56; Mark 14:43-50; Luke 22:47-53; John 18:2-11.

### Deception revealed –

Peter, a follower and disciple, was in the garden with Jesus when He was arrested. He was one of the disciples Jesus ask to watch and pray lest they enter into temptation (Mark 14:33,37,38). When Jesus was led away, Peter followed the crowed as they took Him to the high priests house (Matthew 26:57,58; Mark 15:53,54; Luke 22:54; John 18:15). He stood outside in the courtyard of the house with the servants and the guards of the high priest. He was naturally interested in what was going to happen to Jesus (Matthew 26:58; Mark 14:54; Luke 22:55; John 18:16). He was in the enemies camp and tried to keep a low profile. He was recognized, identified and called out on three occasions (Matthew 26:69-74; Mark 14:66-71; Luke 22:56-60; John 18:17,25-27). Peter denied knowing Jesus each time he was identified. He became so angry that he was continually questioned about his identity and association with Jesus that he swore and cursed (Matthew 26:74; Mark 14:71). Did he think that if he cursed that those who accused him would think that, 'since this man acts this way, he certainly cannot be a follower of Jesus' and then apologize for the mistake and let him alone? We cannot hide our association with God. The people around us may be so consumed with their own lives that they do not recognize our affiliation, but the devil will always know and cause us grief when he can using who he can, even those closest to us. God is always ready to forgive us and return us to His presence when we slip. Peter was so brokenhearted and sorry that he cried (Matthew 26:75; Mark 14:72; Luke 22:62). He was forgiven and Jesus used Peter to build the church and made him a pillar and the chief apostle to the Jews. We are human, we may stumble and even fall. DO NOT LAY THERE! Get back up ask God for forgiveness and strength, dust yourself off continue on in God's grace, mercy and love.

## Heresy –

Saul (Paul) was raised in Tarsus a city rich in knowledge and commerce. His father was a Pharisee, therefore Saul (Paul) was brought up in this doctrine. The Pharisees were a sect of Judaism that thought to adhere so tightly with the law that they excluded the larger truths. They so legalized the laws of God, that they tied down the Jews in their practices and life that they could do nothing without committing a sin against God. Their main purpose of existence was to promote the law. They did not care what political power was in charge as long as the Jewish laws were obeyed and practiced. The Pharisees separated themselves from all others who did not believe as they did, truly deserving the title of 'sect.' Saul was educated in this system. The followers and converts of Jesus were really out of the ways of the law. In his mind then, the followers of Jesus were heretics, the enemy. Being outside the law, they were to be destroyed and the heretics put down. Saul considered it his personal duty to squash the movement where ever he found them (Acts 8:3). He decided to chase those who ran away from the city and destroy them where ever he found them. Saul ask for permission to do the LORD'S work, as he saw it (Acts 9:1,2). Saul hated the new sect that had taken the Jewish community by storm. This unlearned group that followed that rebellious, blasphemous heretic, Jesus, must be destroyed at all cost. He had his letter of authority from the high priest, his sword and his men, he was happily on his way to kill heretics and avenge the breaches of the law. Saul was stopped on the road to Damascus by a bright light and a voice (Acts 9:3-6). We all know who's voice that was, that Saul was filled with the Holy Spirit, his name then being changed to Paul and then was used by Jesus, as chief apostle to the Gentiles to preach the gospel. What started as extreme anger at the breaking of Jewish traditions became a passion to see the undesirables saved by grace through faith in Jesus.

## Lack of perseverance –

The gospel had spread throughout the region, thanks to Paul, Silas, Barnabas and the other apostles. Their church of believers at Antioch (Acts 11:19-21). Barnabas was sent from Jerusalem to examine the churches there and report back to the apostles (Acts 11:22-24). When he discovered the great works of the LORD and the love of the believers toward God, Barnabas went to Tarsus to get Paul and take him to Antioch (Acts 11:25,26). A prophet from Jerusalem came to Antioch and the Spirit of the LORD came upon him and he prophesied that there was going to be a famine throughout all the world. The church took up a collection and sent it to Jerusalem with Barnabas and Paul (Acts 11:27-30). Paul and Barnabas returned to Antioch with John, a nephew of Barnabas' (Acts 12:25; Colossians 4:10). There were prophets and teachers at Antioch, and one day as they were ministering to the LORD and fasting, the Holy Ghost ask for Paul and Barnabas to be separated for a special work. "Now there were in the church that was at Antioch certain prophets and teachers; as Barnabas, and Simeon that was called Niger, and Lucius of Cyrene, and Manaen, which had been brought up with Herod the tetrarch, and Saul. As they ministered to the Lord, and fasted, the Holy Ghost said, Separate me Barnabas and Saul for the work whereunto I have called them. And when they had fasted and prayed, and laid their hands on them, they sent them away." (Acts 13:1-3) They had started their first missionary journey. They took John along with them (Acts 13:4,5). He did not stay long. For some reason he left them at Perga in Pamphylia and returned to Jerusalem (Acts 13:13). There was a council at Jerusalem to determine the doctrinal truths of Paul's teaching and the teaching of the apostles that were in Jerusalem (Acts 15:1-29). Paul and Barnabas attended the council and afterward Paul had a desire to revisit the churches that he had started to see how they were doing. Barnabas wanted to take John with them again. Paul did not want him along. They argued so severely over taking John that they split up and Barnabas went his own way with John. Paul was not sure of John's dedication to the work since he had left them once before (Acts 15:36-39). Paul took Silas and continued his journey (Acts 15:40,41).

# THE PSALMS

Psalms are songs of praise and worship that are meant to be sung with the accompaniment of a small harp called a psaltery. We have modern versions of this instrument but the melodies have been lost through the centuries. What a shame! Some song writers of today have put these beautiful words to music. But, keep in mind, they are not the melodies that the originator had assigned to them. I guess we will have to wait and hear the original Psalm in heaven.

**Example of a psaltery**

This chapter is made up of all the Psalms that contain the words pertaining to anger. I have kept them in their order according in the scriptures. Occasionally you will come across the word ' Selah'. This means, 'to pause and consider this', referring to the previous thought. Also, it was a note to the musician to pause his playing for a short time.

## Psalm 2

1 Why do the heathen rage, and the people imagine a vain thing?
2 The kings of the earth set themselves, and the rulers take counsel together, against the LORD, and against his anointed, saying,
3 Let us break their bands asunder, and cast away their cords from us.
4 He that sitteth in the heavens shall laugh: the Lord shall have them in derision.
5 Then shall he speak unto them in his wrath, and vex them in his sore displeasure.
6 Yet have I set my king upon my holy hill of Zion.
7 I will declare the decree: the LORD hath said unto me, Thou art my Son; this day have I begotten thee.
8 Ask of me, and I shall give thee the heathen for thine inheritance, and the uttermost parts of the earth for thy possession.
9 Thou shalt break them with a rod of iron; thou shalt dash them in pieces like a potter's vessel.
10 Be wise now therefore, O ye kings: be instructed, ye judges of the earth.
11 Serve the LORD with fear, and rejoice with trembling.
12 Kiss the Son, lest he be angry, and ye perish from the way, when his wrath is kindled but a little. Blessed are all they that put their trust in him.

## Psalm 6

1 To the chief Musician on Neginoth upon Sheminith, A Psalm of David. O LORD, rebuke me not in thine anger, neither chasten me in thy hot displeasure.

2 Have mercy upon me, O LORD; for I am weak: O LORD, heal me; for my bones are vexed.

3 My soul is also sore vexed: but thou, O LORD, how long?

4 Return, O LORD, deliver my soul: oh save me for thy mercies' sake.

5 For in death there is no remembrance of thee: in the grave who shall give thee thanks?

6 I am weary with my groaning; all the night make I my bed to swim; I water my couch with my tears.

7 Mine eye is consumed because of grief; it waxeth old because of all mine enemies.

8 Depart from me, all ye workers of iniquity; for the LORD hath heard the voice of my weeping.

9 The LORD hath heard my supplication; the LORD will receive my prayer.

10 Let all mine enemies be ashamed and sore vexed: let them return and be ashamed suddenly.

## Psalm 7

1 Shiggaion of David, which he sang unto the LORD, concerning the words of Cush the Benjamite. O LORD my God, in thee do I put my trust: save me from all them that persecute me, and deliver me:

2 Lest he tear my soul like a lion, rending it in pieces, while there is none to deliver.

3 O LORD my God, if I have done this; if there be iniquity in my hands;

4 If I have rewarded evil unto him that was at peace with me; (yea, I have delivered him that without cause is mine enemy:)

5 Let the enemy persecute my soul, and take it; yea, let him tread down my life upon the earth, and lay mine honour in the dust. Selah.

6 Arise, O LORD, in thine anger, lift up thyself because of the rage of mine enemies: and awake for me to the judgment that thou hast commanded.

7 So shall the congregation of the people compass thee about: for their sakes therefore return thou on high.

8 The LORD shall judge the people: judge me, O LORD, according to my righteousness, and according to mine integrity that is in me.

9 Oh let the wickedness of the wicked come to an end; but establish the just: for the righteous God trieth the hearts and reins.

10 My defence is of God, which saveth the upright in heart.

11 God judgeth the righteous, and God is angry with the wicked every day.

12 If he turn not, he will whet his sword; he hath bent his bow, and made it ready.

13 He hath also prepared for him the instruments of death; he ordaineth his arrows against the persecutors.

14 Behold, he travaileth with iniquity, and hath conceived mischief, and brought forth falsehood.

15 He made a pit, and digged it, and is fallen into the ditch which he made.

16 His mischief shall return upon his own head, and his violent dealing shall come down upon his own pate.

17 I will praise the LORD according to his righteousness: and will sing praise to the name of the LORD most high.

## Psalm 18

1 To the chief Musician, A Psalm of David, the servant of the LORD, who spake unto the LORD the words of this song in the day that the LORD delivered him from the hand of all his

enemies, and from the hand of Saul: And he said, I will love thee, O LORD, my strength.

2 The LORD is my rock, and my fortress, and my deliverer; my God, my strength, in whom I will trust; my buckler, and the horn of my salvation, and my high tower.

3 I will call upon the LORD, who is worthy to be praised: so shall I be saved from mine enemies.

4 The sorrows of death compassed me, and the floods of ungodly men made me afraid.

5 The sorrows of hell compassed me about: the snares of death prevented me.

6 In my distress I called upon the LORD, and cried unto my God: he heard my voice out of his temple, and my cry came before him, even into his ears.

7 Then the earth shook and trembled; the foundations also of the hills moved and were shaken, because he was wroth.

8 There went up a smoke out of his nostrils, and fire out of his mouth devoured: coals were kindled by it.

9 He bowed the heavens also, and came down: and darkness was under his feet.

10 And he rode upon a cherub, and did fly: yea, he did fly upon the wings of the wind.

11 He made darkness his secret place; his pavilion round about him were dark waters and thick clouds of the skies.

12 At the brightness that was before him his thick clouds passed, hail stones and coals of fire.

13 The LORD also thundered in the heavens, and the Highest gave his voice; hail stones and coals of fire.

14 Yea, he sent out his arrows, and scattered them; and he shot out lightnings, and discomfited them.

15 Then the channels of waters were seen, and the foundations of the world were discovered at thy rebuke, O LORD, at the blast of the breath of thy nostrils.

16 He sent from above, he took me, he drew me out of many waters.

17 He delivered me from my strong enemy, and from them which hated me: for they were too strong for me.

18 They prevented me in the day of my calamity: but the LORD was my stay.

19 He brought me forth also into a large place; he delivered me, because he delighted in me.

20 The LORD rewarded me according to my righteousness; according to the cleanness of my hands hath he recompensed me.

21 For I have kept the ways of the LORD, and have not wickedly departed from my God.

22 For all his judgments were before me, and I did not put away his statutes from me.

23 I was also upright before him, and I kept myself from mine iniquity.

24 Therefore hath the LORD recompensed me according to my righteousness, according to the cleanness of my hands in his eyesight.

25 With the merciful thou wilt show thyself merciful; with an upright man thou wilt show thyself upright;

26 With the pure thou wilt show thyself pure; and with the froward thou wilt show thyself froward.

27 For thou wilt save the afflicted people; but wilt bring down high looks.

28 For thou wilt light my candle: the LORD my God will enlighten my darkness.

29 For by thee I have run through a troop; and by my God have I leaped over a wall.

30 As for God, his way is perfect: the word of the LORD is tried: he is a buckler to all those that trust in him.

31 For who is God save the LORD? or who is a rock save our God?

32 It is God that girdeth me with strength, and maketh my way perfect.

33 He maketh my feet like hinds' feet, and setteth me upon my high places.

34 He teacheth my hands to war, so that a bow of steel is broken by mine arms.

35 Thou hast also given me the shield of thy salvation: and thy right hand hath holden me up, and thy gentleness hath made me great.

36 Thou hast enlarged my steps under me, that my feet did not slip.

37 I have pursued mine enemies, and overtaken them: neither did I turn again till they were consumed.

38 I have wounded them that they were not able to rise: they are fallen under my feet.

39 For thou hast girded me with strength unto the battle: thou hast subdued under me those that rose up against me.

40 Thou hast also given me the necks of mine enemies; that I might destroy them that hate me.

41 They cried, but there was none to save them: even unto the LORD, but he answered them not.

42 Then did I beat them small as the dust before the wind: I did cast them out as the dirt in the streets.

43 Thou hast delivered me from the strivings of the people; and thou hast made me the head of the heathen: a people whom I have not known shall serve me.

44 As soon as they hear of me, they shall obey me: the strangers shall submit themselves unto me.

45 The strangers shall fade away, and be afraid out of their close places.

46 The LORD liveth; and blessed be my rock; and let the God of my salvation be exalted.

47 It is God that avengeth me, and subdueth the people under me.

48 He delivereth me from mine enemies: yea, thou liftest me up above those that rise up against me: thou hast delivered me from the violent man.

49 Therefore will I give thanks unto thee, O LORD, among the heathen, and sing praises unto thy name.

50 Great deliverance giveth he to his king; and showeth mercy to his anointed, to David, and to his seed for evermore.

## Psalm 21

1 To the chief Musician, A Psalm of David. The king shall joy in thy strength, O LORD; and in thy salvation how greatly shall he rejoice!

2 Thou hast given him his heart's desire, and hast not withholden the request of his lips. Selah.

3 For thou preventest him with the blessings of goodness: thou settest a crown of pure gold on his head.

4 He asked life of thee, and thou gavest it him, even length of days for ever and ever.

5 His glory is great in thy salvation: honour and majesty hast thou laid upon him.

6 For thou hast made him most blessed for ever: thou hast made him exceeding glad with thy countenance.

7 For the king trusteth in the LORD, and through the mercy of the most High he shall not be moved.

8 Thine hand shall find out all thine enemies: thy right hand shall find out those that hate thee.

9 Thou shalt make them as a fiery oven in the time of thine anger: the LORD shall swallow them up in his wrath, and the fire shall devour them.

10 Their fruit shalt thou destroy from the earth, and their seed from among the children of men.

11 For they intended evil against thee: they imagined a mischievous device, which they are not able to perform.

12 Therefore shalt thou make them turn their back, when thou shalt make ready thine arrows upon thy strings against the face of them.

13 Be thou exalted, LORD, in thine own strength: so will we sing and praise thy power.

## Psalm 27

1 A Psalm of David. The LORD is my light and my salvation; whom shall I fear? the LORD is the strength of my life; of whom shall I be afraid?

2 When the wicked, even mine enemies and my foes, came upon me to eat up my flesh, they stumbled and fell.

3 Though an host should encamp against me, my heart shall not fear: though war should rise against me, in this will I be confident.

4 One thing have I desired of the LORD, that will I seek after; that I may dwell in the house of the LORD all the days of my life, to behold the beauty of the LORD, and to inquire in his temple.

5 For in the time of trouble he shall hide me in his pavilion: in the secret of his tabernacle shall he hide me; he shall set me up upon a rock.

6 And now shall mine head be lifted up above mine enemies round about me: therefore will I offer in his tabernacle sacrifices of joy; I will sing, yea, I will sing praises unto the LORD.

7 Hear, O LORD, when I cry with my voice: have mercy also upon me, and answer me.

8 When thou saidst, Seek ye my face; my heart said unto thee, Thy face, LORD, will I seek.

9 Hide not thy face far from me; put not thy servant away in anger: thou hast been my help; leave me not, neither forsake me, O God of my salvation.

10 When my father and my mother forsake me, then the LORD will take me up.

11 Teach me thy way, O LORD, and lead me in a plain path, because of mine enemies.

12 Deliver me not over unto the will of mine enemies: for false witnesses are risen up against me, and such as breathe out cruelty.

13 I had fainted, unless I had believed to see the goodness of the LORD in the land of the living.

14 Wait on the LORD: be of good courage, and he shall strengthen thine heart: wait, I say, on the LORD.

## Psalm 30

1 A Psalm and Song at the dedication of the house of David. I will extol thee, O LORD; for thou hast lifted me up, and hast not made my foes to rejoice over me.

2 O LORD my God, I cried unto thee, and thou hast healed me.

3 O LORD, thou hast brought up my soul from the grave: thou hast kept me alive, that I should not go down to the pit.

4 Sing unto the LORD, O ye saints of his, and give thanks at the remembrance of his holiness.

5 For his anger endureth but a moment; in his favour is life: weeping may endure for a night, but joy cometh in the morning.

6 And in my prosperity I said, I shall never be moved.

7 LORD, by thy favour thou hast made my mountain to stand strong: thou didst hide thy face, and I was troubled.

8 I cried to thee, O LORD; and unto the LORD I made supplication.

9 What profit is there in my blood, when I go down to the pit? Shall the dust praise thee? shall it declare thy truth?

10 Hear, O LORD, and have mercy upon me: LORD, be thou my helper.

11 Thou hast turned for me my mourning into dancing: thou hast put off my sackcloth, and girded me with gladness;

12 To the end that my glory may sing praise to thee, and not be silent. O LORD my God, I will give thanks unto thee for ever.

## Psalm 37

1 A Psalm of David. Fret not thyself because of evildoers, neither be thou envious against the workers of iniquity.

2 For they shall soon be cut down like the grass, and wither as the green herb.

3 Trust in the LORD, and do good; so shalt thou dwell in the land, and verily thou shalt be fed.

4 Delight thyself also in the LORD; and he shall give thee the desires of thine heart.

5 Commit thy way unto the LORD; trust also in him; and he shall bring it to pass.

6 And he shall bring forth thy righteousness as the light, and thy judgment as the noonday.

7 Rest in the LORD, and wait patiently for him: fret not thyself because of him who prospereth in his way, because of the man who bringeth wicked devices to pass.

8 Cease from anger, and forsake wrath: fret not thyself in any wise to do evil.

9 For evildoers shall be cut off: but those that wait upon the LORD, they shall inherit the earth.

10 For yet a little while, and the wicked shall not be: yea, thou shalt diligently consider his place, and it shall not be.

11 But the meek shall inherit the earth; and shall delight themselves in the abundance of peace.

12 The wicked plotteth against the just, and gnasheth upon him with his teeth.

13 The Lord shall laugh at him: for he seeth that his day is coming.

14 The wicked have drawn out the sword, and have bent their bow, to cast down the poor and needy, and to slay such as be of upright conversation.

15 Their sword shall enter into their own heart, and their bows shall be broken.

16 A little that a righteous man hath is better than the riches of many wicked.

17 For the arms of the wicked shall be broken: but the LORD upholdeth the righteous.

18 The LORD knoweth the days of the upright: and their inheritance shall be for ever.

19 They shall not be ashamed in the evil time: and in the days of famine they shall be satisfied.

20 But the wicked shall perish, and the enemies of the LORD shall be as the fat of lambs: they shall consume; into smoke shall they consume away.

21 The wicked borroweth, and payeth not again: but the righteous showeth mercy, and giveth.

22 For such as be blessed of him shall inherit the earth; and they that be cursed of him shall be cut off.

23 The steps of a good man are ordered by the LORD: and he delighteth in his way.

24 Though he fall, he shall not be utterly cast down: for the LORD upholdeth him with his hand.

25 I have been young, and now am old; yet have I not seen the righteous forsaken, nor his seed begging bread.

26 He is ever merciful, and lendeth; and his seed is blessed.

27 Depart from evil, and do good; and dwell for evermore.

28 For the LORD loveth judgment, and forsaketh not his saints; they are preserved for ever: but the seed of the wicked shall be cut off.

29 The righteous shall inherit the land, and dwell therein for ever.

30 The mouth of the righteous speaketh wisdom, and his tongue talketh of judgment.

31 The law of his God is in his heart; none of his steps shall slide.

32 The wicked watcheth the righteous, and seeketh to slay him.

33 The LORD will not leave him in his hand, nor condemn him when he is judged.

34 Wait on the LORD, and keep his way, and he shall exalt thee to inherit the land: when the wicked are cut off, thou shalt see it.

35 I have seen the wicked in great power, and spreading himself like a green bay tree.

36 Yet he passed away, and, lo, he was not: yea, I sought him, but he could not be found.

37 Mark the perfect man, and behold the upright: for the end of that man is peace.

38 But the transgressors shall be destroyed together: the end of the wicked shall be cut off.

39 But the salvation of the righteous is of the LORD: he is their strength in the time of trouble.

40 And the LORD shall help them, and deliver them: he shall deliver them from the wicked, and save them, because they trust in him.

## Psalm 38

1 A Psalm of David, to bring to remembrance. O LORD, rebuke me not in thy wrath: neither chasten me in thy hot displeasure.

2 For thine arrows stick fast in me, and thy hand presseth me sore.

3 There is no soundness in my flesh because of thine anger; neither is there any rest in my bones because of my sin.

4 For mine iniquities are gone over mine head: as an heavy burden they are too heavy for me.

5 My wounds stink and are corrupt because of my foolishness.

6 I am troubled; I am bowed down greatly; I go mourning all the day long.

7 For my loins are filled with a loathsome disease: and there is no soundness in my flesh.

8 I am feeble and sore broken: I have roared by reason of the disquietness of my heart.

9 Lord, all my desire is before thee; and my groaning is not hid from thee.

10 My heart panteth, my strength faileth me: as for the light of mine eyes, it also is gone from me.

11 My lovers and my friends stand aloof from my sore; and my kinsmen stand afar off.

12 They also that seek after my life lay snares for me: and they that seek my hurt speak mischievous things, and imagine deceits all the day long.

13 But I, as a deaf man, heard not; and I was as a dumb man that openeth not his mouth.

14 Thus I was as a man that heareth not, and in whose mouth are no reproofs.

15 For in thee, O LORD, do I hope: thou wilt hear, O Lord my God.

16 For I said, Hear me, lest otherwise they should rejoice over me: when my foot slippeth, they magnify themselves against me.

17 For I am ready to halt, and my sorrow is continually before me.

18 For I will declare mine iniquity; I will be sorry for my sin.

19 But mine enemies are lively, and they are strong: and they that hate me wrongfully are multiplied.

20 They also that render evil for good are mine adversaries; because I follow the thing that good is.

21 Forsake me not, O LORD: O my God, be not far from me.

22 Make haste to help me, O Lord my salvation.

## Psalm 46

1 To the chief Musician for the sons of Korah, A Song upon Alamoth. God is our refuge and strength, a very present help in trouble.

2 Therefore will not we fear, though the earth be removed, and though the mountains be carried into the midst of the sea;

3 Though the waters thereof roar and be troubled, though the mountains shake with the swelling thereof. Selah.

4 There is a river, the streams whereof shall make glad the city of God, the holy place of the tabernacles of the most High.

5 God is in the midst of her; she shall not be moved: God shall help her, and that right early.

6 The heathen raged, the kingdoms were moved: he uttered his voice, the earth melted.

7 The LORD of hosts is with us; the God of Jacob is our refuge. Selah.

8 Come, behold the works of the LORD, what desolations he hath made in the earth.

9 He maketh wars to cease unto the end of the earth; he breaketh the bow, and cutteth the spear in sunder; he burneth the chariot in the fire.

10 Be still, and know that I am God: I will be exalted among the heathen, I will be exalted in the earth.

11 The LORD of hosts is with us; the God of Jacob is our refuge. Selah.

## Psalm 55

1 To the chief Musician on Neginoth, Maschil, A Psalm of David. Give ear to my prayer, O God; and hide not thyself from my supplication.

2 Attend unto me, and hear me: I mourn in my complaint, and make a noise;

3 Because of the voice of the enemy, because of the oppression of the wicked: for they cast iniquity upon me, and in wrath they hate me.

4 My heart is sore pained within me: and the terrors of death are fallen upon me.

5 Fearfulness and trembling are come upon me, and horror hath overwhelmed me.

6 And I said, Oh that I had wings like a dove! for then would I fly away, and be at rest.

7 Lo, then would I wander far off, and remain in the wilderness. Selah.

8 I would hasten my escape from the windy storm and tempest.

9 Destroy, O Lord, and divide their tongues: for I have seen violence and strife in the city.

10 Day and night they go about it upon the walls thereof: mischief also and sorrow are in the midst of it.

11 Wickedness is in the midst thereof: deceit and guile depart not from her streets.

12 For it was not an enemy that reproached me; then I could have borne it: neither was it he that hated me that did magnify himself against me; then I would have hid myself from him:

13 But it was thou, a man mine equal, my guide, and mine acquaintance.

14 We took sweet counsel together, and walked unto the house of God in company.

15 Let death seize upon them, and let them go down quick into hell: for wickedness is in their dwellings, and among them.

16 As for me, I will call upon God; and the LORD shall save me.

17 Evening, and morning, and at noon, will I pray, and cry aloud: and he shall hear my voice.

18 He hath delivered my soul in peace from the battle that was against me: for there were many with me.

19 God shall hear, and afflict them, even he that abideth of old. Selah. Because they have no changes, therefore they fear not God.

20 He hath put forth his hands against such as be at peace with him: he hath broken his covenant.

21 The words of his mouth were smoother than butter, but war was in his heart: his words were softer than oil, yet were they drawn swords.

22 Cast thy burden upon the LORD, and he shall sustain thee: he shall never suffer the righteous to be moved.

23 But thou, O God, shalt bring them down into the pit of destruction: bloody and deceitful men shall not live out half their days; but I will trust in thee.

## Psalm 56

1 To the chief Musician upon Jonathelemrechokim, Michtam of David, when the Philistines took him in Gath. Be merciful unto me, O God: for man would swallow me up; he fighting daily oppresseth me.

2 Mine enemies would daily swallow me up: for they be many that fight against me, O thou most High.

3 What time I am afraid, I will trust in thee.

4 In God I will praise his word, in God I have put my trust; I will not fear what flesh can do unto me.

5 Every day they wrest my words: all their thoughts are against me for evil.

6 They gather themselves together, they hide themselves, they mark my steps, when they wait for my soul.

7 Shall they escape by iniquity? in thine anger cast down the people, O God.

8 Thou tellest my wanderings: put thou my tears into thy bottle: are they not in thy book?

9 When I cry unto thee, then shall mine enemies turn back: this I know; for God is for me.

10 In God will I praise his word: in the LORD will I praise his word.

11 In God have I put my trust: I will not be afraid what man can do unto me.

12 Thy vows are upon me, O God: I will render praises unto thee.

13 For thou hast delivered my soul from death: wilt not thou deliver my feet from falling, that I may walk before God in the light of the living?

## Psalm 58

1 To the chief Musician, Altaschith, Michtam of David. Do ye indeed speak righteousness, O congregation? do ye judge uprightly, O ye sons of men?

2 Yea, in heart ye work wickedness; ye weigh the violence of your hands in the earth.

3 The wicked are estranged from the womb: they go astray as soon as they be born, speaking lies.

4 Their poison is like the poison of a serpent: they are like the deaf adder that stoppeth her ear;

5 Which will not hearken to the voice of charmers, charming never so wisely.

6 Break their teeth, O God, in their mouth: break out the great teeth of the young lions, O LORD.

7 Let them melt away as waters which run continually: when he bendeth his bow to shoot his arrows, let them be as cut in pieces.

8 As a snail which melteth, let every one of them pass away: like the untimely birth of a woman, that they may not see the sun.

9 Before your pots can feel the thorns, he shall take them away as with a whirlwind, both living, and in his wrath.

10 The righteous shall rejoice when he seeth the vengeance: he shall wash his feet in the blood of the wicked.

11 So that a man shall say, Verily there is a reward for the righteous: verily he is a God that judgeth in the earth.

## Psalm 59

1 To the chief Musician, Altaschith, Michtam of David; when Saul sent, and they watched the house to kill him. Deliver me from mine enemies, O my God: defend me from them that rise up against me.

2 Deliver me from the workers of iniquity, and save me from bloody men.

3 For, lo, they lie in wait for my soul: the mighty are gathered against me; not for my transgression, nor for my sin, O LORD.

4 They run and prepare themselves without my fault: awake to help me, and behold.

5 Thou therefore, O LORD God of hosts, the God of Israel, awake to visit all the heathen: be not merciful to any wicked transgressors. Selah.

6 They return at evening: they make a noise like a dog, and go round about the city.

7 Behold, they belch out with their mouth: swords are in their lips: for who, say they, doth hear?

8 But thou, O LORD, shalt laugh at them; thou shalt have all the heathen in derision.

9 Because of his strength will I wait upon thee: for God is my defence.

10 The God of my mercy shall prevent me: God shall let me see my desire upon mine enemies.

11 Slay them not, lest my people forget: scatter them by thy power; and bring them down, O Lord our shield.

12 For the sin of their mouth and the words of their lips let them even be taken in their pride: and for cursing and lying which they speak.

13 Consume them in wrath, consume them, that they may not be: and let them know that God ruleth in Jacob unto the ends of the earth. Selah.

14 And at evening let them return; and let them make a noise like a dog, and go round about the city.

15 Let them wander up and down for meat, and grudge if they be not satisfied.

16 But I will sing of thy power; yea, I will sing aloud of thy mercy in the morning: for thou hast been my defence and refuge in the day of my trouble.

17 Unto thee, O my strength, will I sing: for God is my defence, and the God of my mercy.

## Psalm 60

1 To the chief Musician upon Shushaneduth, Michtam of David, to teach; when he strove with Aramnaharaim and with Aramzobah, when Joab returned, and smote of Edom in the valley of salt twelve thousand. O God, thou hast cast us off, thou hast scattered us, thou hast been displeased; O turn thyself to us again.

2 Thou hast made the earth to tremble; thou hast broken it: heal the breaches thereof; for it shaketh.

3 Thou hast showed thy people hard things: thou hast made us to drink the wine of astonishment.

4 Thou hast given a banner to them that fear thee, that it may be displayed because of the truth. Selah.

5 That thy beloved may be delivered; save with thy right hand, and hear me.

6 God hath spoken in his holiness; I will rejoice, I will divide Shechem, and mete out the valley of Succoth.

7 Gilead is mine, and Manasseh is mine; Ephraim also is the strength of mine head; Judah is my lawgiver;

8 Moab is my washpot; over Edom will I cast out my shoe: Philistia, triumph thou because of me.

9 Who will bring me into the strong city? who will lead me into Edom?

10 Wilt not thou, O God, which hadst cast us off? and thou, O God, which didst not go out with our armies?

11 Give us help from trouble: for vain is the help of man.

12 Through God we shall do valiantly: for he it is that shall tread down our enemies.

## Psalm 69

1 To the chief Musician upon Shoshannim, A Psalm of David. Save me, O God; for the waters are come in unto my soul.

2 I sink in deep mire, where there is no standing: I am come into deep waters, where the floods overflow me.

3 I am weary of my crying: my throat is dried: mine eyes fail while I wait for my God.

4 They that hate me without a cause are more than the hairs of mine head: they that would destroy me, being mine enemies wrongfully, are mighty: then I restored that which I took not away.

5 O God, thou knowest my foolishness; and my sins are not hid from thee.

6 Let not them that wait on thee, O Lord GOD of hosts, be ashamed for my sake: let not those that seek thee be confounded for my sake, O God of Israel.

7 Because for thy sake I have borne reproach; shame hath covered my face.

8 I am become a stranger unto my brethren, and an alien unto my mother's children.

9 For the zeal of thine house hath eaten me up; and the reproaches of them that reproached thee are fallen upon me.

10 When I wept, and chastened my soul with fasting, that was to my reproach.

11 I made sackcloth also my garment; and I became a proverb to them.

12 They that sit in the gate speak against me; and I was the song of the drunkards.

13 But as for me, my prayer is unto thee, O LORD, in an acceptable time: O God, in the multitude of thy mercy hear me, in the truth of thy salvation.

14 Deliver me out of the mire, and let me not sink: let me be delivered from them that hate me, and out of the deep waters.

15 Let not the waterflood overflow me, neither let the deep swallow me up, and let not the pit shut her mouth upon me.

16 Hear me, O LORD; for thy lovingkindness is good: turn unto me according to the multitude of thy tender mercies.

17 And hide not thy face from thy servant; for I am in trouble: hear me speedily.

18 Draw nigh unto my soul, and redeem it: deliver me because of mine enemies.

19 Thou hast known my reproach, and my shame, and my dishonour: mine adversaries are all before thee.

20 Reproach hath broken my heart; and I am full of heaviness: and I looked for some to take pity, but there was none; and for comforters, but I found none.

21 They gave me also gall for my meat; and in my thirst they gave me vinegar to drink.

22 Let their table become a snare before them: and that which should have been for their welfare, let it become a trap.

23 Let their eyes be darkened, that they see not; and make their loins continually to shake.

24 Pour out thine indignation upon them, and let thy wrathful anger take hold of them.

25 Let their habitation be desolate; and let none dwell in their tents.

26 For they persecute him whom thou hast smitten; and they talk to the grief of those whom thou hast wounded.

27 Add iniquity unto their iniquity: and let them not come into thy righteousness.

28 Let them be blotted out of the book of the living, and not be written with the righteous.

29 But I am poor and sorrowful: let thy salvation, O God, set me up on high.

30 I will praise the name of God with a song, and will magnify him with thanksgiving.

31 This also shall please the LORD better than an ox or bullock that hath horns and hoofs.

32 The humble shall see this, and be glad: and your heart shall live that seek God.

33 For the LORD heareth the poor, and despiseth not his prisoners.

34 Let the heaven and earth praise him, the seas, and everything that moveth therein.

35 For God will save Zion, and will build the cities of Judah: that they may dwell there, and have it in possession.

36 The seed also of his servants shall inherit it: and they that love his name shall dwell therein.

## Psalm 74

1 Maschil of Asaph. O God, why hast thou cast us off forever? why doth thine anger smoke against the sheep of thy pasture?

2 Remember thy congregation, which thou hast purchased of old; the rod of thine inheritance, which thou hast redeemed; this mount Zion, wherein thou hast dwelt.

3 Lift up thy feet unto the perpetual desolations; even all that the enemy hath done wickedly in the sanctuary.

4 Thine enemies roar in the midst of thy congregations; they set up their ensigns for signs.

5 A man was famous according as he had lifted up axes upon the thick trees.

6 But now they break down the carved work thereof at once with axes and hammers.

7 They have cast fire into thy sanctuary, they have defiled by casting down the dwelling place of thy name to the ground.

8 They said in their hearts, Let us destroy them together: they have burned up all the synagogues of God in the land.

9 We see not our signs: there is no more any prophet: neither is there among us any that knoweth how long.

10 O God, how long shall the adversary reproach? shall the enemy blaspheme thy name forever?

11 Why withdrawest thou thy hand, even thy right hand? pluck it out of thy bosom.

12 For God is my King of old, working salvation in the midst of the earth.

13 Thou didst divide the sea by thy strength: thou brakest the heads of the dragons in the waters.

14 Thou brakest the heads of leviathan in pieces, and gavest him to be meat to the people inhabiting the wilderness.

15 Thou didst cleave the fountain and the flood: thou driedst up mighty rivers.

16 The day is thine, the night also is thine: thou hast prepared the light and the sun.

17 Thou hast set all the borders of the earth: thou hast made summer and winter.

18 Remember this, that the enemy hath reproached, O LORD, and that the foolish people have blasphemed thy name.

19 O deliver not the soul of thy turtledove unto the multitude of the wicked: forget not the congregation of thy poor for ever.

20 Have respect unto the covenant: for the dark places of the earth are full of the habitations of cruelty.

21 O let not the oppressed return ashamed: let the poor and needy praise thy name.

22 Arise, O God, plead thine own cause: remember how the foolish man reproacheth thee daily.

23 Forget not the voice of thine enemies: the tumult of those that rise up against thee increaseth continually.

## Psalm 76

1 To the chief Musician on Neginoth, A Psalm or Song of Asaph. In Judah is God known: his name is great in Israel.

2 In Salem also is his tabernacle, and his dwelling place in Zion.

3 There brake he the arrows of the bow, the shield, and the sword, and the battle. Selah.

4 Thou art more glorious and excellent than the mountains of prey.

5 The stouthearted are spoiled, they have slept their sleep: and none of the men of might have found their hands.

6 At thy rebuke, O God of Jacob, both the chariot and horse are cast into a dead sleep.

7 Thou, even thou, art to be feared: and who may stand in thy sight when once thou art angry?

8 Thou didst cause judgment to be heard from heaven; the earth feared, and was still,

9 When God arose to judgment, to save all the meek of the earth. Selah.

10 Surely the wrath of man shall praise thee: the remainder of wrath shalt thou restrain.

11 Vow, and pay unto the LORD your God: let all that be round about him bring presents unto him that ought to be feared.

12 He shall cut off the spirit of princes: he is terrible to the kings of the earth.

## Psalm 77

1 To the chief Musician, to Jeduthun, A Psalm of Asaph. I cried unto God with my voice, even unto God with my voice; and he gave ear unto me.

2 In the day of my trouble I sought the Lord: my sore ran in the night, and ceased not: my soul refused to be comforted.

3 I remembered God, and was troubled: I complained, and my spirit was overwhelmed. Selah.

4 Thou holdest mine eyes waking: I am so troubled that I cannot speak.

5 I have considered the days of old, the years of ancient times.

6 I call to remembrance my song in the night: I commune with mine own heart: and my spirit made diligent search.

7 Will the Lord cast off for ever? and will he be favourable no more?

8 Is his mercy clean gone for ever? doth his promise fail for evermore?

9 Hath God forgotten to be gracious? hath he in anger shut up his tender mercies? Selah.

10 And I said, This is my infirmity: but I will remember the years of the right hand of the most High.

11 I will remember the works of the LORD: surely I will remember thy wonders of old.

12 I will meditate also of all thy work, and talk of thy doings.

13 Thy way, O God, is in the sanctuary: who is so great a God as our God?

14 Thou art the God that doest wonders: thou hast declared thy strength among the people.

15 Thou hast with thine arm redeemed thy people, the sons of Jacob and Joseph. Selah.

16 The waters saw thee, O God, the waters saw thee; they were afraid: the depths also were troubled.

17 The clouds poured out water: the skies sent out a sound: thine arrows also went abroad.

18 The voice of thy thunder was in the heaven: the lightnings lightened the world: the earth trembled and shook.

19 Thy way is in the sea, and thy path in the great waters, and thy footsteps are not known.

20 Thou leddest thy people like a flock by the hand of Moses and Aaron.

## Psalm 78

1 Maschil of Asaph. Give ear, O my people, to my law: incline your ears to the words of my mouth.

2 I will open my mouth in a parable: I will utter dark sayings of old:

3 Which we have heard and known, and our fathers have told us.

4 We will not hide them from their children, showing to the generation to come the praises of the LORD, and his strength, and his wonderful works that he hath done.

5 For he established a testimony in Jacob, and appointed a law in Israel, which he commanded our fathers, that they should make them known to their children:

6 That the generation to come might know them, even the children which should be born; who should arise and declare them to their children:

7 That they might set their hope in God, and not forget the works of God, but keep his commandments:

8 And might not be as their fathers, a stubborn and rebellious generation; a generation that set not their heart aright, and whose spirit was not stedfast with God.

9 The children of Ephraim, being armed, and carrying bows, turned back in the day of battle.

10 They kept not the covenant of God, and refused to walk in his law;

11 And forgat his works, and his wonders that he had showed them.

12 Marvellous things did he in the sight of their fathers, in the land of Egypt, in the field of Zoan.

13 He divided the sea, and caused them to pass through; and he made the waters to stand as an heap.

14 In the daytime also he led them with a cloud, and all the night with a light of fire.

15 He clave the rocks in the wilderness, and gave them drink as out of the great depths.

16 He brought streams also out of the rock, and caused waters to run down like rivers.

17 And they sinned yet more against him by provoking the most High in the wilderness.

18 And they tempted God in their heart by asking meat for their lust.

19 Yea, they spake against God; they said, Can God furnish a table in the wilderness?

20 Behold, he smote the rock, that the waters gushed out, and the streams overflowed; can he give bread also? can he provide flesh for his people?

21 Therefore the LORD heard this, and was wroth: so a fire was kindled against Jacob, and anger also came up against Israel;

22 Because they believed not in God, and trusted not in his salvation:

23 Though he had commanded the clouds from above, and opened the doors of heaven,

24 And had rained down manna upon them to eat, and had given them of the corn of heaven.

25 Man did eat angels' food: he sent them meat to the full.

26 He caused an east wind to blow in the heaven: and by his power he brought in the south wind.

27 He rained flesh also upon them as dust, and feathered fowls like as the sand of the sea:

28 And he let it fall in the midst of their camp, round about their habitations.

29 So they did eat, and were well filled: for he gave them their own desire;

30 They were not estranged from their lust. But while their meat was yet in their mouths,

31 The wrath of God came upon them, and slew the fattest of them, and smote down the chosen men of Israel.

32 For all this they sinned still, and believed not for his wondrous works.

33 Therefore their days did he consume in vanity, and their years in trouble.

34 When he slew them, then they sought him: and they returned and inquired early after God.

35 And they remembered that God was their rock, and the high God their redeemer.

36 Nevertheless they did flatter him with their mouth, and they lied unto him with their tongues.

37 For their heart was not right with him, neither were they stedfast in his covenant.

38 But he, being full of compassion, forgave their iniquity, and destroyed them not: yea, many a time turned he his anger away, and did not stir up all his wrath.

39 For he remembered that they were but flesh; a wind that passeth away, and cometh not again.

40 How oft did they provoke him in the wilderness, and grieve him in the desert!

41 Yea, they turned back and tempted God, and limited the Holy One of Israel.

42 They remembered not his hand, nor the day when he delivered them from the enemy.

43 How he had wrought his signs in Egypt, and his wonders in the field of Zoan:

44 And had turned their rivers into blood; and their floods, that they could not drink.

45 He sent divers sorts of flies among them, which devoured them; and frogs, which destroyed them.

46 He gave also their increase unto the caterpillar, and their labour unto the locust.

47 He destroyed their vines with hail, and their sycamore trees with frost.

48 He gave up their cattle also to the hail, and their flocks to hot thunderbolts.

49 He cast upon them the fierceness of his anger, wrath, and indignation, and trouble, by sending evil angels among them.

50 He made a way to his anger; he spared not their soul from death, but gave their life over to the pestilence;

51 And smote all the firstborn in Egypt; the chief of their strength in the tabernacles of Ham:

52 But made his own people to go forth like sheep, and guided them in the wilderness like a flock.

53 And he led them on safely, so that they feared not: but the sea overwhelmed their enemies.

54 And he brought them to the border of his sanctuary, even to this mountain, which his right hand had purchased.

55 He cast out the heathen also before them, and divided them an inheritance by line, and made the tribes of Israel to dwell in their tents.

56 Yet they tempted and provoked the most high God, and kept not his testimonies:

57 But turned back, and dealt unfaithfully like their fathers: they were turned aside like a deceitful bow.

58 For they provoked him to anger with their high places, and moved him to jealousy with their graven images.

59 When God heard this, he was wroth, and greatly abhorred Israel:

60 So that he forsook the tabernacle of Shiloh, the tent which he placed among men;

61 And delivered his strength into captivity, and his glory into the enemy's hand.

62 He gave his people over also unto the sword; and was wroth with his inheritance.

63 The fire consumed their young men; and their maidens were not given to marriage.

64 Their priests fell by the sword; and their widows made no lamentation.

65 Then the Lord awaked as one out of sleep, and like a mighty man that shoutethy reason of wine.

66 And he smote his enemies in the hinder parts: he put them to a perpetual reproach.

67 Moreover he refused the tabernacle of Joseph, and chose not the tribe of Ephraim:

68 But chose the tribe of Judah, the mount Zion which he loved.

69 And he built his sanctuary like high palaces, like the earth which he hath established for ever.

70 He chose David also his servant, and took him from the sheepfolds:

71 From following the ewes great with young he brought him to feed Jacob his people, and Israel his inheritance.

72 So he fed them according to the integrity of his heart; and guided them by the skilfulness of his hands.

## Psalm 79

1 A Psalm of Asaph. O God, the heathen are come into thine inheritance; thy holy temple have they defiled; they have laid Jerusalem on heaps.

2 The dead bodies of thy servants have they given to be meat unto the fowls of the heaven, the flesh of thy saints unto the beasts of the earth.

3 Their blood have they shed like water round about Jerusalem; and there was none to bury them.

4 We are become a reproach to our neighbours, a scorn and derision to them that are round about us.

5 How long, LORD? wilt thou be angry for ever? shall thy jealousy burn like fire?

6 Pour out thy wrath upon the heathen that have not known thee, and upon the kingdoms that have not called upon thy name.

7 For they have devoured Jacob, and laid waste his dwelling place.

8 O remember not against us former iniquities: let thy tender mercies speedily prevent us: for we are brought very low.

9 Help us, O God of our salvation, for the glory of thy name: and deliver us, and purge away our sins, for thy name's sake.

10 Wherefore should the heathen say, Where is their God? let him be known among the heathen in our sight by the revenging of the blood of thy servants which is shed.

11 Let the sighing of the prisoner come before thee; according to the greatness of thy power preserve thou those that are appointed to die;

12 And render unto our neighbours sevenfold into their bosom their reproach, wherewith they have reproached thee, O Lord.

13 So we thy people and sheep of thy pasture will give thee thanks for ever: we will show forth thy praise to all generations.

## Psalm 80

1 To the chief Musician upon Shoshannimeduth, A Psalm of Asaph. Give ear, O Shepherd of Israel, thou that leadest Joseph like a flock; thou that dwellest between the cherubims, shine forth.

2 Before Ephraim and Benjamin and Manasseh stir up thy strength, and come and save us.

3 Turn us again, O God, and cause thy face to shine; and we shall be saved.

4 O LORD God of hosts, how long wilt thou be angry against the prayer of thy people?

5 Thou feedest them with the bread of tears; and givest them tears to drink in great measure.

6 Thou makest us a strife unto our neighbours: and our enemies laugh among themselves.

7 Turn us again, O God of hosts, and cause thy face to shine; and we shall be saved.

8 Thou hast brought a vine out of Egypt: thou hast cast out the heathen, and planted it.

9 Thou preparedst room before it, and didst cause it to take deep root, and it filled the land.

10 The hills were covered with the shadow of it, and the boughs thereof were like the goodly cedars.

11 She sent out her boughs unto the sea, and her branches unto the river.

12 Why hast thou then broken down her hedges, so that all they which pass by the way do pluck her?

13 The boar out of the wood doth waste it, and the wild beast of the field doth devour it.

14 Return, we beseech thee, O God of hosts: look down from heaven, and behold, and visit this vine;

15 And the vineyard which thy right hand hath planted, and the branch that thou madest strong for thyself.

16 It is burned with fire, it is cut down: they perish at the rebuke of thy countenance.

17 Let thy hand be upon the man of thy right hand, upon the son of man whom thou madest strong for thyself.

18 So will not we go back from thee: quicken us, and we will call upon thy name.

19 Turn us again, O LORD God of hosts, cause thy face to shine; and we shall be saved.

## Psalm 85

1 To the chief Musician, A Psalm for the sons of Korah. LORD, thou hast been favourable unto thy land: thou hast brought back the captivity of Jacob.

2 Thou hast forgiven the iniquity of thy people, thou hast covered all their sin. Selah.

3 Thou hast taken away all thy wrath: thou hast turned thyself from the fierceness of thine anger.

4 Turn us, O God of our salvation, and cause thine anger toward us to cease.

5 Wilt thou be angry with us for ever? wilt thou draw out thine anger to all generations?

6 Wilt thou not revive us again: that thy people may rejoice in thee?

7 Show us thy mercy, O LORD, and grant us thy salvation.

8 I will hear what God the LORD will speak: for he will speak peace unto his people, and to his saints: but let them not turn again to folly.

9 Surely his salvation is nigh them that fear him; that glory may dwell in our land.

10 Mercy and truth are met together; righteousness and peace have kissed each other.

11 Truth shall spring out of the earth; and righteousness shall look down from heaven.

12 Yea, the LORD shall give that which is good; and our land shall yield her increase.

13 Righteousness shall go before him; and shall set us in the way of his steps.

## Psalm 88

1 A Song or Psalm for the sons of Korah, to the chief Musician upon Mahalath Leannoth, Maschil of Heman the Ezrahite. O LORD God of my salvation, I have cried day and night before thee:

2 Let my prayer come before thee: incline thine ear unto my cry;

3 For my soul is full of troubles: and my life draweth nigh unto the grave.

4 I am counted with them that go down into the pit: I am as a man that hath no strength:

5 Free among the dead, like the slain that lie in the grave, whom thou rememberest no more: and they are cut off from thy hand.

6 Thou hast laid me in the lowest pit, in darkness, in the deeps.

7 Thy wrath lieth hard upon me, and thou hast afflicted me with all thy waves. Selah.

8 Thou hast put away mine acquaintance far from me; thou hast made me an abomination unto them: I am shut up, and I cannot come forth.

9 Mine eye mourneth by reason of affliction: LORD, I have called daily upon thee, I have stretched out my hands unto thee.

10 Wilt thou show wonders to the dead? shall the dead arise and praise thee? Selah.

11 Shall thy lovingkindness be declared in the grave? or thy faithfulness in destruction?

12 Shall thy wonders be known in the dark? and thy righteousness in the land of forgetfulness?

13 But unto thee have I cried, O LORD; and in the morning shall my prayer prevent thee.

14 LORD, why castest thou off my soul? why hidest thou thy face from me?

15 I am afflicted and ready to die from my youth up: while I suffer thy terrors I am distracted.

16 Thy fierce wrath goeth over me; thy terrors have cut me off.

17 They came round about me daily like water; they compassed me about together.

18 Lover and friend hast thou put far from me, and mine acquaintance into darkness.

## Psalm 89

1 Maschil of Ethan the Ezrahite. I will sing of the mercies of the LORD for ever: with my mouth will I make known thy faithfulness to all generations.

2 For I have said, Mercy shall be built up for ever: thy faithfulness shalt thou establish in the very heavens.

3 I have made a covenant with my chosen, I have sworn unto David my servant,

4 Thy seed will I establish for ever, and build up thy throne to all generations. Selah.

5 And the heavens shall praise thy wonders, O LORD: thy faithfulness also in the congregation of the saints.

6 For who in the heaven can be compared unto the LORD? who among the sons of the mighty can be likened unto the LORD?

7 God is greatly to be feared in the assembly of the saints, and to be had in reverence of all them that are about him.

8 O LORD God of hosts, who is a strong LORD like unto thee? or to thy faithfulness round about thee?

9 Thou rulest the raging of the sea: when the waves thereof arise, thou stillest them.

10 Thou hast broken Rahab in pieces, as one that is slain; thou hast scattered thine enemies with thy strong arm.

11 The heavens are thine, the earth also is thine: as for the world and the fulness thereof, thou hast founded them.

12 The north and the south thou hast created them: Tabor and Hermon shall rejoice in thy name.

13 Thou hast a mighty arm: strong is thy hand, and high is thy right hand.

14 Justice and judgment are the habitation of thy throne: mercy and truth shall go before thy face.

15 Blessed is the people that know the joyful sound: they shall walk, O LORD, in the light of thy countenance.

16 In thy name shall they rejoice all the day: and in thy righteousness shall they be exalted.

17 For thou art the glory of their strength: and in thy favour our horn shall be exalted.

18 For the LORD is our defence; and the Holy One of Israel is our king.

19 Then thou spakest in vision to thy holy one, and saidst, I have laid help upon one that is mighty; I have exalted one chosen out of the people.

20 I have found David my servant; with my holy oil have I anointed him:

21 With whom my hand shall be established: mine arm also shall strengthen him.

22 The enemy shall not exact upon him; nor the son of wickedness afflict him.

23 And I will beat down his foes before his face, and plague them that hate him.

24 But my faithfulness and my mercy shall be with him: and in my name shall his horn be exalted.

25 I will set his hand also in the sea, and his right hand in the rivers.

26 He shall cry unto me, Thou art my father, my God, and the rock of my salvation.

27 Also I will make him my firstborn, higher than the kings of the earth.

28 My mercy will I keep for him for evermore, and my covenant shall stand fast with him.

29 His seed also will I make to endure for ever, and his throne as the days of heaven.

30 If his children forsake my law, and walk not in my judgments;

31 If they break my statutes, and keep not my commandments;

32 Then will I visit their transgression with the rod, and their iniquity with stripes.

33 Nevertheless my lovingkindness will I not utterly take from him, nor suffer my faithfulness to fail.

34 My covenant will I not break, nor alter the thing that is gone out of my lips.

35 Once have I sworn by my holiness that I will not lie unto David.

36 His seed shall endure for ever, and his throne as the sun before me.

37 It shall be established for ever as the moon, and as a faithful witness in heaven. Selah.

38 But thou hast cast off and abhorred, thou hast been wroth with thine anointed.

39 Thou hast made void the covenant of thy servant: thou hast profaned his crown by casting it to the ground.

40 Thou hast broken down all his hedges; thou hast brought his strong holds to ruin.

41 All that pass by the way spoil him: he is a reproach to his neighbours.

42 Thou hast set up the right hand of his adversaries; thou hast made all his enemies to rejoice.

43 Thou hast also turned the edge of his sword, and hast not made him to stand in the battle.

44 Thou hast made his glory to cease, and cast his throne down to the ground.

45 The days of his youth hast thou shortened: thou hast covered him with shame. Selah.

46 How long, LORD? wilt thou hide thyself for ever? shall thy wrath burn like fire?

47 Remember how short my time is: wherefore hast thou made all men in vain?

48 What man is he that liveth, and shall not see death? shall he deliver his soul from the hand of the grave? Selah.

49 Lord, where are thy former lovingkindnesses, which thou swarest unto David in thy truth?

50 Remember, Lord, the reproach of thy servants; how I do bear in my bosom the reproach of all the mighty people;

51 Wherewith thine enemies have reproached, O LORD; wherewith they have reproached the footsteps of thine anointed.

52 Blessed be the LORD for evermore. Amen, and Amen.

## Psalm 90

1 A Prayer of Moses the man of God. LORD, thou hast been our dwelling place in all generations.

2 Before the mountains were brought forth, or ever thou hadst formed the earth and the world, even from everlasting to everlasting, thou art God.

3 Thou turnest man to destruction; and sayest, Return, ye children of men.

4 For a thousand years in thy sight are but as yesterday when it is past, and as a watch in the night.

5 Thou carriest them away as with a flood; they are as a sleep: in the morning they are like grass which groweth up.

6 In the morning it flourisheth, and groweth up; in the evening it is cut down, and withereth.

7 For we are consumed by thine anger, and by thy wrath are we troubled.

8 Thou hast set our iniquities before thee, our secret sins in the light of thy countenance.

9 For all our days are passed away in thy wrath: we spend our years as a tale that is told.

10 The days of our years are threescore years and ten; and if by reason of strength they be fourscore years, yet is their strength labour and sorrow; for it is soon cut off, and we fly away.

11 Who knoweth the power of thine anger? even according to thy fear, so is thy wrath.

12 So teach us to number our days, that we may apply our hearts unto wisdom.

13 Return, O LORD, how long? and let it repent thee concerning thy servants.

14 O satisfy us early with thy mercy; that we may rejoice and be glad all our days.

15 Make us glad according to the days wherein thou hast afflicted us, and the years wherein we have seen evil.

16 Let thy work appear unto thy servants, and thy glory unto their children.

17 And let the beauty of the LORD our God be upon us: and establish thou the work of our hands upon us; yea, the work of our hands establish thou it.

## Psalm 95

1 O come, let us sing unto the LORD: let us make a joyful noise to the rock of our salvation.

2 Let us come before his presence with thanksgiving, and make a joyful noise unto him with psalms.

3 For the LORD is a great God, and a great King above all gods.

4 In his hand are the deep places of the earth: the strength of the hills is his also.

5 The sea is his, and he made it: and his hands formed the dry land.

6 O come, let us worship and bow down: let us kneel before the LORD our maker.

7 For he is our God; and we are the people of his pasture, and the sheep of his hand. To day if ye will hear his voice,

8 Harden not your heart, as in the provocation, and as in the day of temptation in the wilderness:

9 When your fathers tempted me, proved me, and saw my work.

10 Forty years long was I grieved with this generation, and said, It is a people that do err in their heart, and they have not known my ways:

11 Unto whom I sware in my wrath that they should not enter into my rest.

## Psalm 102

1 A Prayer of the afflicted, when he is overwhelmed, and poureth out his complaint before the LORD. Hear my prayer, O LORD, and let my cry come unto thee.

2 Hide not thy face from me in the day when I am in trouble; incline thine ear unto me: in the day when I call answer me speedily.

3 For my days are consumed like smoke, and my bones are burned as an hearth.

4 My heart is smitten, and withered like grass; so that I forget to eat my bread.

5 By reason of the voice of my groaning my bones cleave to my skin.

6 I am like a pelican of the wilderness: I am like an owl of the desert.

7 I watch, and am as a sparrow alone upon the house top.

8 Mine enemies reproach me all the day; and they that are mad against me are sworn against me.

9 For I have eaten ashes like bread, and mingled my drink with weeping,

10 Because of thine indignation and thy wrath: for thou hast lifted me up, and cast me down.

11 My days are like a shadow that declineth; and I am withered like grass.

12 But thou, O LORD, shalt endure for ever; and thy remembrance unto all generations.

13 Thou shalt arise, and have mercy upon Zion: for the time to favour her, yea, the set time, is come.

14 For thy servants take pleasure in her stones, and favour the dust thereof.

15 So the heathen shall fear the name of the LORD, and all the kings of the earth thy glory.

16 When the LORD shall build up Zion, he shall appear in his glory.

17 He will regard the prayer of the destitute, and not despise their prayer.

18 This shall be written for the generation to come: and the people which shall be created shall praise the LORD.

19 For he hath looked down from the height of his sanctuary; from heaven did the LORD behold the earth;

20 To hear the groaning of the prisoner; to loose those that are appointed to death;

21 To declare the name of the LORD in Zion, and his praise in Jerusalem;

22 When the people are gathered together, and the kingdoms, to serve the LORD.

23 He weakened my strength in the way; he shortened my days.

24 I said, O my God, take me not away in the midst of my days: thy years are throughout all generations.

25 Of old hast thou laid the foundation of the earth: and the heavens are the work of thy hands.

26 They shall perish, but thou shalt endure: yea, all of them shall wax old like a garment; as a vesture shalt thou change them, and they shall be changed:

27 But thou art the same, and thy years shall have no end.

28 The children of thy servants shall continue, and their seed shall be established before thee.

## Psalm 103

1 A Psalm of David. Bless the LORD, O my soul: and all that is within me, bless his holy name.

2 Bless the LORD, O my soul, and forget not all his benefits:

3 Who forgiveth all thine iniquities; who healeth all thy diseases;

4 Who redeemeth thy life from destruction; who crowneth thee with lovingkindness and tender mercies;

5 Who satisfieth thy mouth with good things; so that thy youth is renewed like the eagle's.

6 The LORD executeth righteousness and judgment for all that are oppressed.

7 He made known his ways unto Moses, his acts unto the children of Israel.

8 The LORD is merciful and gracious, slow to anger, and plenteous in mercy.

9 He will not always chide: neither will he keep his anger for ever.

10 He hath not dealt with us after our sins; nor rewarded us according to our iniquities.

11 For as the heaven is high above the earth, so great is his mercy toward them that fear him.

12 As far as the east is from the west, so far hath he removed our transgressions from us.

13 Like as a father pitieth his children, so the LORD pitieth them that fear him.

14 For he knoweth our frame; he remembereth that we are dust.

15 As for man, his days are as grass: as a flower of the field, so he flourisheth.

16 For the wind passeth over it, and it is gone; and the place thereof shall know it no more.

17 But the mercy of the LORD is from everlasting to everlasting upon them that fear him, and his righteousness unto children's children;

18 To such as keep his covenant, and to those that remember his commandments to do them.

19 The LORD hath prepared his throne in the heavens; and his kingdom ruleth over all.

20 Bless the LORD, ye his angels, that excel in strength, that do his commandments, hearkening unto the voice of his word.

21 Bless ye the LORD, all ye his hosts; ye ministers of his, that do his pleasure.

22 Bless the LORD, all his works in all places of his dominion: bless the LORD, O my soul.

## Psalm 106

1 Praise ye the LORD. O give thanks unto the LORD; for he is good: for his mercy endureth for ever.

2 Who can utter the mighty acts of the LORD? who can show forth all his praise?

3 Blessed are they that keep judgment, and he that doeth righteousness at all times.

4 Remember me, O LORD, with the favour that thou bearest unto thy people: O visit me with thy salvation;

5 That I may see the good of thy chosen, that I may rejoice in the gladness of thy nation, that I may glory with thine inheritance.

6 We have sinned with our fathers, we have committed iniquity, we have done wickedly.

7 Our fathers understood not thy wonders in Egypt; they remembered not the multitude of thy mercies; but provoked him at the sea, even at the Red sea.

8 Nevertheless he saved them for his name's sake, that he might make his mighty power to be known.

9 He rebuked the Red sea also, and it was dried up: so he led them through the depths, as through the wilderness.

10 And he saved them from the hand of him that hated them, and redeemed them from the hand of the enemy.

11 And the waters covered their enemies: there was not one of them left.

12 Then believed they his words; they sang his praise.

13 They soon forgat his works; they waited not for his counsel:

14 But lusted exceedingly in the wilderness, and tempted God in the desert.

15 And he gave them their request; but sent leanness into their soul.

16 They envied Moses also in the camp, and Aaron the saint of the LORD.

17 The earth opened and swallowed up Dathan, and covered the company of Abiram.

18 And a fire was kindled in their company; the flame burned up the wicked.

19 They made a calf in Horeb, and worshipped the molten image.

20 Thus they changed their glory into the similitude of an ox that eateth grass.

21 They forgat God their saviour, which had done great things in Egypt;

22 Wondrous works in the land of Ham, and terrible things by the Red sea.

23 Therefore he said that he would destroy them, had not Moses his chosen stood before him in the breach, to turn away his wrath, lest he should destroy them.

24 Yea, they despised the pleasant land, they believed not his word:

25 But murmured in their tents, and hearkened not unto the voice of the LORD.

26 Therefore he lifted up his hand against them, to overthrow them in the wilderness:

27 To overthrow their seed also among the nations, and to scatter them in the lands.

28 They joined themselves also unto Baalpeor, and ate the sacrifices of the dead.

29 Thus they provoked him to anger with their inventions: and the plague brake in upon them.

30 Then stood up Phinehas, and executed judgment: and so the plague was stayed.

31 And that was counted unto him for righteousness unto all generations for evermore.

32 They angered him also at the waters of strife, so that it went ill with Moses for their sakes:

33 Because they provoked his spirit, so that he spake unadvisedly with his lips.

34 They did not destroy the nations, concerning whom the LORD commanded them:

35 But were mingled among the heathen, and learned their works.

36 And they served their idols: which were a snare unto them.

37 Yea, they sacrificed their sons and their daughters unto devils,

38 And shed innocent blood, even the blood of their sons and of their daughters, whom they sacrificed unto the idols of Canaan: and the land was polluted with blood.

39 Thus were they defiled with their own works, and went a whoring with their own inventions.

40 Therefore was the wrath of the LORD kindled against his people, insomuch that he abhorred his own inheritance.

41 And he gave them into the hand of the heathen; and they that hated them ruled over them.

42 Their enemies also oppressed them, and they were brought into subjection under their hand.

43 Many times did he deliver them; but they provoked him with their counsel, and were brought low for their iniquity.

44 Nevertheless he regarded their affliction, when he heard their cry:

45 And he remembered for them his covenant, and repented according to the multitude of his mercies.

46 He made them also to be pitied of all those that carried them captives.

47 Save us, O LORD our God, and gather us from among the heathen, to give thanks unto thy holy name, and to triumph in thy praise.

48 Blessed be the LORD God of Israel from everlasting to everlasting: and let all the people say, Amen. Praise ye the LORD.

## Psalm 110

1 A Psalm of David. The LORD said unto my Lord, Sit thou at my right hand, until I make thine enemies thy footstool.

2 The LORD shall send the rod of thy strength out of Zion: rule thou in the midst of thine enemies.

3 Thy people shall be willing in the day of thy power, in the beauties of holiness from the womb of the morning: thou hast the dew of thy youth.

4 The LORD hath sworn, and will not repent, Thou art a priest for ever after the order of Melchizedek.

5 The Lord at thy right hand shall strike through kings in the day of his wrath.

6 He shall judge among the heathen, he shall fill the places with the dead bodies; he shall wound the heads over many countries.

7 He shall drink of the brook in the way: therefore shall he lift up the head.

## Psalm 124

1 A Song of degrees of David. If it had not been the LORD who was on our side, now may Israel say;

2 If it had not been the LORD who was on our side, when men rose up against us:

3 Then they had swallowed us up quick, when their wrath was kindled against us:

4 Then the waters had overwhelmed us, the stream had gone over our soul:

5 Then the proud waters had gone over our soul.

6 Blessed be the LORD, who hath not given us as a prey to their teeth.

7 Our soul is escaped as a bird out of the snare of the fowlers: the snare is broken, and we are escaped.

8 Our help is in the name of the LORD, who made heaven and earth.

## Psalm 138

1 A Psalm of David. I will praise thee with my whole heart: before the gods will I sing praise unto thee.

2 I will worship toward thy holy temple, and praise thy name for thy lovingkindness and for thy truth: for thou hast magnified thy word above all thy name.

3 In the day when I cried thou answeredst me, and strengthenedst me with strength in my soul.

4 All the kings of the earth shall praise thee, O LORD, when they hear the words of thy mouth.

5 Yea, they shall sing in the ways of the LORD: for great is the glory of the LORD.

6 Though the LORD be high, yet hath he respect unto the lowly: but the proud he knoweth afar off.

7 Though I walk in the midst of trouble, thou wilt revive me: thou shalt stretch forth thine hand against the wrath of mine enemies, and thy right hand shall save me.

8 The LORD will perfect that which concerneth me: thy mercy, O LORD, endureth for ever: forsake not the works of thine own hands.

## Psalm 145

1 David's Psalm of praise. I will extol thee, my God, O king; and I will bless thy name for ever and ever.

2 Every day will I bless thee; and I will praise thy name for ever and ever.

3 Great is the LORD, and greatly to be praised; and his greatness is unsearchable.

4 One generation shall praise thy works to another, and shall declare thy mighty acts.

5 I will speak of the glorious honour of thy majesty, and of thy wondrous works.

6 And men shall speak of the might of thy terrible acts: and I will declare thy greatness.

7 They shall abundantly utter the memory of thy great goodness, and shall sing of thy righteousness.

8 The LORD is gracious, and full of compassion; slow to anger, and of great mercy.

9 The LORD is good to all: and his tender mercies are over all his works.

10 All thy works shall praise thee, O LORD; and thy saints shall bless thee.

11 They shall speak of the glory of thy kingdom, and talk of thy power;

12 To make known to the sons of men his mighty acts, and the glorious majesty of his kingdom.

13 Thy kingdom is an everlasting kingdom, and thy dominion endureth throughout all generations.

14 The LORD upholdeth all that fall, and raiseth up all those that be bowed down.

15 The eyes of all wait upon thee; and thou givest them their meat in due season.

16 Thou openest thine hand, and satisfiest the desire of every living thing.

17 The LORD is righteous in all his ways, and holy in all his works.

18 The LORD is nigh unto all them that call upon him, to all that call upon him in truth.

19 He will fulfil the desire of them that fear him: he also will hear their cry, and will save them.

20 The LORD preserveth all them that love him: but all the wicked will he destroy.

21 My mouth shall speak the praise of the LORD: and let all flesh bless his holy name for ever and ever.

# THE PROVERBS

Proverbs are short pithy sayings that express a great truth. They teach practical and spiritual wisdom. The book of Proverbs best describes its purpose and contents. "To know wisdom and instruction; to perceive the words of understanding; to receive the instruction of wisdom, justice, and judgment, and equity; to give subtlety to the simple, to the young man knowledge and discretion. A wise man will hear, and will increase learning; and a man of understanding shall attain unto wise counsels: to understand a proverb, and the interpretation; the words of the wise, and their dark sayings. The fear of the LORD is the beginning of knowledge: but fools despise wisdom and instruction." (Proverbs 1:2-7) There are some proverbs that deal with anger. We have seen thus far, anger is a part of human existence. Therefore, it must be dealt with on all levels and understood so that we mere mortals can get control of it and not let it control us.

I have listed the proverbs here in their order as they appear in the scriptures. Read and pray over them and allow God to use them to teach you how to bring your own temper into submission. You must always control anger and never let anger control you.

## Proverbs 6 - Adultery and Dishonor

32 But whoso committeth adultery with a woman lacketh understanding: he that doeth it destroyeth his own soul.

33 A wound and dishonour shall he get; and his reproach shall not be wiped away.

34 For jealousy is the rage of a man: therefore he will not spare in the day of vengeance.

35 He will not regard any ransom; neither will he rest content, though thou givest many gifts.

## Proverbs 11 - Righteousness verses Wickedness

3 The integrity of the upright shall guide them: but the perverseness of transgressors shall destroy them.

4 Riches profit not in the day of wrath: but righteousness delivereth from death.

5 The righteousness of the perfect shall direct his way: but the wicked shall fall by his own wickedness.

6 The righteousness of the upright shall deliver them: but transgressors shall be taken in their own naughtiness.

23 The desire of the righteous is only good: but the expectation of the wicked is wrath.

## Proverbs 12 - Foolish verses the Prudent Man

16 A fool's wrath is presently known: but a prudent man covereth shame.

## Proverbs 14 - Wise man verses the Foolish

16 A wise man feareth, and departeth from evil: but the fool rageth, and is confident.

17 He that is soon angry dealeth foolishly: and a man of wicked devices is hated.

29 He that is slow to wrath is of great understanding: but he that is hasty of spirit exalteth folly.

35 The king's favour is toward a wise servant: but his wrath is against him that causeth shame.

## Proverbs 15 - The Control of Anger & The Promotion of Peace

1 A soft answer turneth away wrath: but grievous words stir up anger.

18 A wrathful man stirreth up strife: but he that is slow to anger appeaseth strife.

## Proverbs 16 - A Man With An Even Temper is A Powerful Man

14 The wrath of a king is as messengers of death: but a wise man will pacify it.

32 He that is slow to anger is better than the mighty; and he that ruleth his spirit than he that taketh a city.

## Proverbs 19 - Discretion

11 The discretion of a man deferreth his anger; and it is his glory to pass over a transgression.

12 The king's wrath is as the roaring of a lion; but his favour is as dew upon the grass.

19 A man of great wrath shall suffer punishment: for if thou deliver him, yet thou must do it again.

## Proverbs 20 - Consumption of Alcohol & Meddling in Others Affairs

1 Wine is a mocker, strong drink is raging: and whosoever is deceived thereby is not wise.

2 The fear of a king is as the roaring of a lion: whoso provoketh him to anger sinneth against his own soul.

3 It is an honour for a man to cease from strife: but every fool will be meddling.

## Proverbs 21 – A Gift in Secret & A Proud and Haughty Scorner

14 A gift in secret pacifieth anger: and a reward in the bosom strong wrath.

19 It is better to dwell in the wilderness, than with a contentious and an angry woman.

24 Proud and haughty scorner is his name, who dealeth in proud wrath.

## Proverbs 22 – The Sower of Iniquity; Friendship of an Angry Man

8 He that soweth iniquity shall reap vanity: and the rod of his anger shall fail.

24 Make no friendship with an angry man; and with a furious man thou shalt not go:

25 Lest thou learn his ways, and get a snare to thy soul.

## Proverbs 24 – Rejoice not when thine enemy falleth

17 Rejoice not when thine enemy falleth, and let not thine heart be glad when he stumbleth:

18 Lest the LORD see it, and it displease him, and he turn away his wrath from him.

## Proverbs 25 – A Concealed or Slandering Tongue Produces Anger

23 The north wind driveth away rain: so doth an angry countenance a backbiting tongue.

Note: This verse is better translated as, "As the north wind bringeth forth or produces rain, so does a concealed or slandering tongue produce anger." according to Jameison-Faussett-Brown Commentaries.

## Proverbs 27 - A Fool's Wrath & Envy

3 A stone is heavy, and the sand weighty; but a fool's wrath is heavier than them both.

4 Wrath is cruel, and anger is outrageous; but who is able to stand before envy?

## Proverbs 29 - Scornful Men, A Wise Man and An Angry Man

8 Scornful men bring a city into a snare: but wise men turn away wrath.

9 If a wise man contendeth with a foolish man, whether he rage or laugh, there is no rest.

22 An angry man stirreth up strife, and a furious man aboundeth in transgression.

## Proverbs 30 - Wrath Brings Strife

33 Surely the churning of milk bringeth forth butter, and the wringing of the nose bringeth forth blood: so the forcing of wrath bringeth forth strife.

# CONCLUSION

Anger is common to all creatures. Animals will fight to protect their territory, food or mates. Have you ever watched two dogs playing with a rope toy? Soon one will become more aggressive than the other, then the war is on. They will forget about the toy and begin to chew on each other. This behavior is not exclusive to the animal kingdom. Observe children on the playground or participating in a sporting event. At first, all is well, then one team starts to dominate the other. Either on the field, by having a higher score or psychologically, by taunting the weaker players. The stress created in these situations will cause the dominated persons to become angry and lash out aggressively. Now we have a fight. The children are not the only ones to exhibit this behavior. Watch any football or basketball game and you will surely see arguments and fights. Sometimes, I think hockey is three periods of fighting broken up by short time spans of skating. As has been stated many times in this book, anger itself is not bad. The way you choose to express it or react to it can definitely be.

God can get very angry. He has destroyed this earth once that is recorded in the Old Testament. Has He destroyed the earth before the flood of Noah? Do we really know what happened to the dinosaurs? Did God destroy the earth with an asteroid as the 'experts' suggest? Is that why Genesis 1:2 reads, "And the earth was without form, and void; and darkness was upon the face of the deep. And the Spirit of God moved upon the face of the waters." We cannot ascribe to God the attribute of being a kindly, old Grandfather that will overlook the errors of His children as long as we believe that He flooded the earth and saved only Noah and his family. God is merciful, patient and kind, but He has His limits. The chapter discussing the anger of God listed many reasons that God was taken to His breaking point and acted against the sinners, and His people when they did not obey. God knew that the people He created and gave free will would be too weak willed to serve Him as He required. When a prophet was with them they would obey His will, when the prophet died they would turn from His ways and serve idols or other gods. The downfall and casting to earth of Satan created a serious conflict between God's kingdom and the one that Satan had created for himself on earth. When God would tell His people something through a prophet, Satan would come right behind and contradict God's instruction. Our LORD had planned for this situation from the beginning. When the appointed time arrived, He created Jesus. "But when the fulness of the time was come, God sent forth his Son, made of a woman, made under the law, To redeem them that were under the law, that we might receive the adoption of sons." (Galatians 4:4,5) John writes, "For God so loved the world, that he gave his only begotten Son, that whosoever believeth in him should not perish, but have everlasting life." (John 3:16) Along with salvation, God introduced grace to the earth through Jesus. No longer are we required to live as Moses had instructed, following all the laws and performing the sacrifices daily. When we fall, by giving into sin and disobeying God, we now can go directly to the Father, ask and receive forgiveness. "My little children, these things write I unto you, that ye sin not. And if any man sin, we have an advocate with the Father, Jesus Christ the righteous:" (1

John 2:1) We should all be glad that God loves us enough to get angry! Without God's love and anger we would not have needed the birth, life example, crucifixion and resurrection of Jesus. We would not have salvation and the promise of a heavenly home for eternity. God's anger and punishment is always justified and well deserved by those whom He afflicts.

The anger of man on the other hand can be and usually is vindictive, petty and generally self-serving. We have seen many reasons the Bible characters became angry, some good, some bad, and some downright silly. In the chapter dealing with the Bible character's anger, we have seen these people get angry for reasons ranging from a neighbor who did not want to sell his land extending to a younger brother conning the older out of his birthright and blessing. Then there was the petty response of a king who divorces his wife just because she chose to maintain her feminine proprieties and not to be paraded in front of her husband and his drunk companions as if she were a highly prized show pony. This study caused me to examine myself and evaluate the situations that have made me angry. I revisited the list that I had made at the beginning of this study of the things that made me angry. They were petty and self-serving. Most of the situations were just inconveniences and others were self-centered. I recognized that there was a pattern that developed before I blew and if I could break that pattern I could control my anger. First, I get impatient with the situation or person. Secondly, I lose interest in the present situation or person speaking. Thirdly, I want to be doing anything else other than what I am. Finally, frustration sets in because I have no control of the present. Therefore, in order to regain control, I explode! This scares the person away or into silence. At this time I am not really in control, things have went too far, therefore, the cursing, hurtful words flow and urge to fight or flight are completely in control of me. What should be painfully obvious now, is that if God is love and the controlling force in your anger situation is hateful, then the devil is the one in control at that moment! This is the quickest way for the devil to get a foothold in your life. Even if you have all your spiritual armor on, anger is a very big crack. The devil can see it a mile away and will attack you at that point every time.

Anger, in the light of God's word, is a waste of emotion and energy. To be angry at anything except the perversion of God's word and the lost souls that could have been added to the kingdom of God is a **total** waste of time and effort! What did you really accomplished by getting angry? What did you prove? Let's say you totally let go and showed your rage and anger, you rant and rave, swear and throw things. Is the problem or situation solved? Are those around you more agreeable to your way of thinking? All you have accomplished is to make a show of yourself and give all those around something to talk about! The neighbors will talk, too! They will tell of your exploits for many years. What if the police were called? What about the hole that is in the wall because you picked up the most handy item and threw it, missing your intended target (probably because you're spouse ducked out of the way). You have created yourself, or someone, some unnecessary work. The wall needs to be repaired. Did you speak some pretty colorful and hurtful words? Now you have grieved God and you need to apologize to Him and ask His forgiveness. Thank God, He will always forgive, but be prepared to feel a little alienation from Him for a short while. He does punish those who He loves, for their sins. "And ye have forgotten the exhortation which speaketh unto you as unto children, My son, despise not thou the chastening of the Lord, nor faint when thou art rebuked of him: For whom the Lord loveth he chasteneth, and scourgeth every son whom he receiveth. If ye endure chastening, God dealeth with you as with sons; for what son is he whom the father chasteneth not?" (Hebrews 12:5-7)

I ask you to examine yourself. I pray that you do. Why did you get angry? Was it reasonable, selfish or petty? Only you can answer these questions about your own life. No one else can answer them for you. You do have an advantage that I did not. If you have read this book through then you know what made the Biblical characters loose it. Compare your emotions and the situations that made you angry to theirs. I pray that God will give your insight into yourself and that you will, with God's help, change that which is ungodly and not scriptural. "And be renewed in the spirit of your mind; And that ye put on the new man, which after God is created in righteousness and true holiness." (Ephesians 4:23,24) The 'putting on of the new man' is a conscience and prayerful effort. It is not easy!! We learned to be tough by acting tough; we learned to be friends by acting friendly. We learned to be ungodly by embracing the old sinful nature and acting sinful. To put on the new man we now have to act Godly and make that our habit of living. This change starts in our minds, we are renewed in the spirit of our minds by putting Godly thoughts in there and learning God's ways. Read the Bible, pray daily, fast at least once a week and attend a church where you can be with other God fearing people. "Finally, brethren, whatsoever things are true, whatsoever things are honest, whatsoever things are just, whatsoever things are pure, whatsoever things are lovely, whatsoever things are of good report; if there be any virtue, and if there be any praise, think on these things." (Philippians 4:8) Renew your mind! We have Christ put on us when we believe and are baptized. "For as many of you as have been baptized into Christ have put on Christ." (Galatians 3:27) God has done His part by giving us the power to live according to His will, He gave us the Holy Spirit, and He gave us instructions on how to live a life pleasing to Him, the Bible. Our responsibility is to study and become knowledgeable of His word and then live it. "Study to show thyself approved unto God, a workman that needeth not to be ashamed, rightly dividing the word of truth." (2 Timothy 2:15) Knowing is one thing, living it daily is quite another. "... having done all, to stand." (Ephesians 6:13)

Let me say again to be angry is not a sin, but how you express that anger or react to someone's can very definitely be. Anger expressed in the right way can be used by God to bring glory and honor to Himself, but only if you do not sin in the expression of your anger. King Ahasuerus became angry at his queen, Vashti, and God used the occasion to make Esther the queen and save the Jews from Haman's evil plan of extermination. All because Mordecai exhibited his anger the proper way.

There are those who would stir your anger to benefit their own ends. The revolutionaries for example are at this date calling for you to get angry an turn that anger against the very people that would help you. They would gain anarchy and then be able to take over our great nation and turn it into something that no American would recognize. As a case in point I want to introduce you to Francis Fox Piven. Francis Fox Piven calls for violence - She's considered by many as the grandmother of using the American welfare state to implement revolution. Make people dependent on the government, overload the government rolls, and once government services become unsustainable, the people will rise up, overthrow the oppressive capitalist system, and finally create income equality. Collapse the system and create a new one. That's the simplified version of Frances Fox Piven's philosophy originally put forth in the pages of The Nation in the 60s. Now, as the new year ball drops, Piven is at it again, ringing in 2011 with renewed calls for revolution.

In a chilling and almost unbelievable editorial again in The Nation ("Mobilizing the Jobless," January 10/17, 2011 edition), she calls on the jobless to rise up in a violent show of solidarity and force. As before, those calls are dripping with language of class struggle. Language she and her late husband Richard Cloward made popular in the 60s. "So where are the angry crowds, the demonstrations, sit-ins and unruly mobs?" she writes. "After all, the injustice is apparent. Working people are losing their homes and their pensions while robber-baron CEOs report renewed profits and windfall bonuses. Shouldn't the unemployed be on the march? Why aren't they demanding enhanced safety net protections and big initiatives to generate jobs?" Those are the questions that frame what can best be called a roadmap for revolution. And it's not long before those questions give way to directions. The first instruction: get angry. "Before people can mobilize for collective action, they have to develop a proud and angry identity and a set of claims that go with that identity," she writes. "They have to go from being hurt and ashamed to being angry and indignant." And along with anger must come a denunciation of personal responsibility. Instead, workers must realize that others have put them in their current, uneasy situation: "The out-of-work have to stop blaming themselves for their hard times and turn their anger on the bosses, the bureaucrats or the politicians who are in fact responsible."

Only then, once their rage has been properly stoked, can the angry take action. And when they do, she says, the "protesters need targets."

For Piven, the best "targets" are the people or organizations "capable of making some kind of response to angry demands." Regular demands, notice, just won't do. No, people must be fired up and not easily deterred. Angry and not quickly placated. It's a concoction Piven has seen recently in other countries — countries such as England and Greece, which she uses as models for American unrest: An effective movement of the unemployed will have to look something like the strikes and riots that have spread across Greece in response to the austerity measures forced on the Greek government by the European Union, or like the student protests that recently spread with lightning speed across England in response to the prospect of greatly increased school fees.

This is very much demonic and should be avoided at all costs. Reverend Doctor Martin Luther King advised in his "I Have a Dream" speech given August 28, 1963. "But there is something that I must say to my people, who stand on the warm threshold which leads into the palace of justice: In the process of gaining our rightful place, we must not be guilty of wrongful deeds. Let us not seek to satisfy our thirst for freedom by drinking from the cup of bitterness and hatred. We must forever conduct our struggle on the high plane of dignity and discipline. We must not allow our creative protest to degenerate into physical violence. Again and again, we must rise to the majestic heights of meeting physical force with soul force."

Anger heated to the extreme and turned into violence is not the Godly way nor should it ever be the intelligent human being way. Even in the movie, "Star Wars", Yoda warned, "Fear is the path to the dark side. Fear leads to anger. Anger leads to hate. Hate leads to suffering." Learn to control your anger through Godly, righteous ways. These are all taught in the Bible and were referred to in this book. God is love, therefore anyone that would direct you to hate must be serving the devil. The decision as to which path to walk is yours and yours alone. I pray that you choose to go with God. Let us end where we began. "Be ye angry, and sin not: let not the sun go down upon your wrath: Neither give place to the devil." (Ephesians 4:26,27)

**May God bless and keep you through your time on this earth. As the old blessing says, "May you be in heaven one hour before the devil knows you are dead."**

# BIBLE REFERENCES

1. Cruelty - (murder – Exodus 20:13) Genesis 49:5-7; Zechariah 10:3

2. Idolatry - Exodus 20:2-6; 32:4,10-12,33; Numbers 22:22; Deuteronomy 4:25-31; 6:13-15; 7:1-6; 9:7,8,12-22; 29:10-28; 32:28,29; Judges. 2, 3:5-23, 26-31; 10:6,7; 1Ki. 11:4-10; 14:7-11, 15; 15:29,30; 2Ki. 17:7-24; 21:1-16; 22:13,17; 23:26,27; 2Chr. 24:18; 25:14-16; 28:1-25; 33:1-17; 34:21,23-25; Jeremiah 7:29-31; 11:17; 15:4,14; 17:1-4; 25:5-7; 32:26-35; 44:1-8; 52:1-3; Ezekiel 6:11-14; 7:20-22;8:15-18;16 (God judges Israel for their idolatry); Ezekiel 36:16-20; Hosea 8:4-6; Zephaniah 1:18; 3:8; God judges Aholibah for serving other gods (whoring) Ezekiel 23:22-30

3. Hardness of heart – Deuteronomy 29:19; Mark 3:1-5; Romans 2:5; Hebrews 3:7-19 (stiff-necked) – Exodus 32:9; 33:3,5; 34:9; Deuteronomy 9:6,13; 10:16; 2 Chronicles 30:8; Acts 7:51

4. Those who would attempt to destroy God's anointed people – Psalms 21; 37; Isaiah 7:1-9; Habakkuk 3:13; Nehemiah 4:1-6

5. Doubting God's ability to sustain His people – Psalms 78:1-22; Deuteronomy 1:29-36

6. God's people's iniquities – Psalms 90:8 (Exposed by the light of God's countenance) - Ezekiel 22:1-12; Daniel 9:16

7. Sinners - (these verses refer to Babylon and her king also to those who would not accept or serve God) - Isaiah 13

8. When God's people get full, comfortable and forget God. - Hos 13:1-11 (Prayer for redemption) – Hosea 14:1-3; Deuteronomy 6:1-16; Ezekiel 22:12

9. Cruelty to and between God's people – Isaiah 14:1-6 (brother against brother) - Amos 1, 2

10. Doubting God's ability to use you as you are when called – Exodus 3; 4:1-14

11. Complaining – Numbers 11:1-3; 16:41-48

12. Mutiny, speaking against God's chosen ones or authority – Numbers 12; 16:12-35

13. Israel mixing with the nation they were to displace – Numbers 25:1-13; Ezra. 9:10-14; 10:10-14

14. Doubting God can deliver on His promises – Numbers 13:17-33; 14:1-4; 32:7-15; Deuteronomy 9:22-29

15. People who would lead Israel away from God to idols – 1 Kings 16:1-33; 21:17-27; 22:51-53; 2 Kings 13:2,3

16. Disobedience – 2 Samuel 6:1-1; Jeremiah 42:1-18 (Disobedience of Israel) - Lamentations 1;3,5,18,20; 3:42,43; Ezekiel 5:5-14; 20:8,21 (Moses and Aaron struck the rock instead of speaking to the rock) - Numbers 20:7-13 (Nadab and Abihu offered strange fire to God) - Leviticus 10:1-6 (A warning to obey God) - Deuteronomy 11:13-17 (Saul lost the kingdom because he did not obey God) - 1 Samuel 15:8,9; 28:18 (Jerusalem disobeyed God and turned away from Him) - Zephaniah 3:1-7; Zechariah 7:8-14; Ephesians 5:3-6) (Onan wasted his seed) - Genesis 38:6-10; Joshua 7:1

17. Pride – (Satan's sin) - Isaiah 14:9-14; Ezekiel 28:11-19 (David was provoked by Satan to number the people of Israel) 1 Chronicles 21:1,7; 27:23,24). (David's sin, listening to Satan, became pride in his heart) - 2 Samuel 24: 1-10

(Pride can make you think things are owed to you) – 2 Chronicles 32:25,26 Proverbs dealing with pride - Proverbs 8:13; 11:2; 13:10; 14:3; 16:18; 29:23 (The pride of Ephraim and the whole world to be judged) - Isaiah 28:1-22

18. Turning away from God (Backsliding) – Isaiah 1:4; (Hezekiah re-establishes the temple and the service of the Levites 2 Chronicles 29:3-11) (An exhortation to return to the Lord) - Zechariah 1:1-6 (Backsliders) – Isaiah 42:17-25; Jeremiah 2:13; 3:6-8; 7;8:5-19

19. Those who despise the Word of God – Isaiah 5:20-25; 2 Chronicles 36:15-17

20. Pride mixed with arrogance – Isaiah 9:8-12; 10:12-19

21. Hypocrites – Isaiah 9:13-17; 10:5,6; Job 8:11-15; 13:15,16; 15:34,35; 20:4,5; 27:8; 34:29,30; 36:13,14 (Reward for righteousness) - Isaiah 33:13-16 (Definition) - Isaiah 29:13; Matthew 15:7,8; Mark 7:6-8 (Admonishment to the leaders of the Israelites) - Matthew 23:2-7, 13-31; Luke 11:39-52 (Hypocrites make up their own rules) - 1Timothy 4:1-5

22. Wickedness (the wicked) – Isaiah 9:18-21; Jeremiah 30:23,24; 33:4,5; Jonah 1:2; Job 10:14-16; Deuteronomy 9:4,5; 17:2-5; Nehemiah 9:33-38

23. Those who decree unrighteous decrees, and that write grievousness laws (who make unfair and unjust laws) – Isaiah 10:1-4

24. Rebellious people – (God's curse and blessings for a people who have not turned away from Him completely) - Isaiah 25:7; 29:15; 30:1; Deuteronomy 29:19; Hosea

25. False teaching and teachers – Jeremiah 23:1-4; 2 Peter 2:1

26. False priests and prophets – Jeremiah 23:9-40; Lamentations 4:13-16; Ezekiel 13:1-23; 22:23-31

27. Those who rejoice in the misery and punishment of God's - Ezekiel 25; 35

28. Forsaking His commandments – 2 Chronicles 12:5-12; Ezra. 9:10-14 (Blessings for obedience and curses for disobedience) – Levitcus 26:3-39
29. Making a vow (promise or pledge), then not paying or fulfilling it – Ecclesiastes 5:5,6
30. Afflictions of widows or of fatherless children – Exodus 22:22-24
31. Lust – Numbers 10:31-34; 11:4,34; Psalms 81:12; 106:14; Matthew 5:28; Romans 1:24-27; 6:12; 7:7; 13:14; Galatians 516,17; James 1:14,15; 4:1-5; 1 Peter 4:2,3; 2 Peter 1:4; 1 John 2:16,17
32. Breaking of oaths given in God's name – Joshua 9:3-21
33. Everyone who supports the wicked and hates the Lord – 2 Chronicles 19:2
34. Brothers taking advantage of each other – 2 Chronicles 28:6-13
35. Those who forsake Him – Ezra 8:22; Ezekiel 22:12-14
36. Respect of person – Job 42:7; Ecclesiastes 9:1-3; Matthew 7:1-5; Luke 6:37,38; John 7:24; Romans 2:11; Ephesians. 6:9; Colossians 3:25; James 2:1; 1 Pet. 1:17
37. Dealing unfairly with your neighbor – Hosea 5:10; Deuteronomy 19:14
38. Men who hold the truth in unrighteousness – Romans 1:16-25
39. Those who disobey the truth – Romans 2:4-9
40. Those who persecute God's people – Acts 8:1,3; 9:1-5; 13:9,45-47,50; 17:5-9,13; 1 Thessalonians 2:14-16; Hebrews 10:32-34
41. Those who take the mark of the beast and their leaders – Revelation 13; 14:9-11,18-20; 18:2-20; Joel 3:13-17
42. Those who would destroy God's people – 2 Kings 18:13-19,36; 2 Samuel 22:5-9
43. The rage of the tongue – Hosea 7:16

44. Complaining and dissatisfaction with God's provisions – Exodus 16:2-35; Numbers 11:1-10,31-34
45. Adultery covered up by murder – (David and Bath-Sheba) – 2 Samuel 11:2-27; 12:1-25
46. No Judgment – Isaiah 59:1-16
47. The heathen that is at ease - Zechariah 1:7-17; 2:6-9
48. Covetousness and dealing falsely – Jeremiah 6:9-25; 5:25-31
49. Iniquity – Genesis 6:5-8; Jeremiah 25:12-16; John 3:16,17
50. Dealing by revenge and a spiteful heart – Ezekiel 25:15-17

## What made the Bible characters angry -

1. Injustice - (Esau's anger at Jacob) - Genesis. 25:21-34; 27:41-45 (Samson's father-in-law had given his wife to another) - Judges 14:1-4,7,15-20;15:1-5
2. Jealousy - (Rachel was angry with Jacob because of Leah's fertility) – Genesis 29; 30 (Cain was jealous of Abel because God accepted Abel's offering but rejected his) - Genesis 4:2-8 (Saul was jealous of David because the people said that David was a better warrior than him) – 1 Samuel 18:7,8
3. Self-willed Disobedience – (Simeon and Levi) - Genesis 34:2-31; 49:5-7
4. Other people's obstinacy - (Moses and Pharaoh) – Exodus11:8
5. Impatience and Idolatry – (The impatience of the Israelites) - Exodus.12:35,36; 32:19,22
6. Complaining and dissatisfaction with God's provisions – The people's lust for meat.- Numbers. 11:10, 18-23, 31-34
7. The burden of responsibility – (Moses complained of burden to God) - Numbers 11:11-14,16,17, 24-30
8. Disobedience – (Balaam punished his donkey three times because it veered off the path) - Numbers 22:22-34 (Vashti's refusal of Ahasuerus' summons) - Esther 1:10-12; 2:1 (The goat of the sin offering) - Leviticus 10:16

18; 9:3,15 (Nebuchadnezar and Shadrach, Meshach, and Abednego) - Daniel 3 (The leftover manna) - Exodus 16:16-20 (The Israeli commanders took prisoners) - Numbers 31:14-18 (Daniel in the lion's den) – Daniel 6:1-17

9.  Betrayal – (Balak summoned Balaam) - Numbers 24:10-13 (Sampson's riddle exposed) - Judges 14:12-19 (Joseph's master's wife) - Genesis 39:7-20

10. False Sense of Pride - (The Ephraimites and Gideon) - Judges 8:1-3

11. Insolence and Inconsiderate Attitudes – (Saul, the Ammonites, the men of Jabesh-Gilead) – 1 Samuel 11:1-11

12. Presumptive Attitude of Youth – (Eliab, the oldest brother, and David) – 1 Samuel 17:20-28

13. Treachery – (Saul was angry with Jonathan) – 1 Samuel 20:1-33

14. Shame – (Jonathan was ashamed of Saul) – 1 Samuel 20:32-34

15. Theft – (Micah's neighbors were angry at the warriors of Dan) - Jud. 17; 18 (Laban was angry with Jacob) - Genesis 31:1-42

16. Disappointment – (Ahab was angry with Naboth) – 1 Kings 21:1-4 (Naaman was angry at Elisha) – 2 Kings 5:1-19

17. Loss in a business deal – (The Israelites were angry with Amaziah) – 2 Chronicles 25:5-10,13

18. Working all your life and having nothing – Ecclesiastes 5:14-17; Matthew 6:19,20

19. To appear to be a false prophet – Jonah 3:4,10; 4:1-11

20. Fear ("troubled at his presence") - Genesis 45:1-5

21. Political power grab – 2 Samuel 19:41-43

22. Oppression of God's people – Nehemiah 5:1-13

23. Deceit – (Nebuchadnezzar demanded that the wise men interpret his dream) – Daniel 2:1-13 (The king in the parable had prearranged with certain people to attend the wedding of his son) - Matthew 22:2-10; Luke 14:16-24

24. Loss of property – The prodigal son) - Luke 15:11-32
25. Disobedience of the Mosaic 'law' – Luke 13:10-17; 14:1-6; John 7:21-24
26. God's return and rewarding of His people - Revelation11:18
27. Fear of Holy retribution – Joshua 22:9-33
28. Disobedience to the law (man's law) – (Haman was angry with Mordecai) – Esther 3:1-6; 5:9
29. Presumption of power – (Ahasuerus was angry with Haman) - Esther 7:2-10
30. Justifying yourself rather than justifying God – Job 32; 33
31. Blasphemy – (Jesus proclaims His Godliness in the synagogue) - Luke 4:16-29; Isaiah 61:1,2 (Stephen was falsely accused and stoned to death) – Acts 6:8-15; 7:54-60
32. Loss of job/wealth – Acts 16:16-24; 19:24-28
33. Being rushed to accomplish a purpose – Revelation 12:6-17
34. Suffering an insult – 2 Kings 5:1-14
35. Being told your faults or mistakes – 2 Chronicles 16:7-10; 26:1-21
36. Someone taking advantage of a relative – Genesis 34:1-7; 2 Samuel 13:1-22
37. Unspecified offense – (Pharaoh was angry at his butler and baker) – Genesis 40:1,2; 41:10 (Two of Ahasuerus's guards were angry and conspired to do the king harm) – Esther 2:21(Herod was displeased with Tyre and Sidon) - Acts 12:20
38. Treason – (The Philistine princes did not trust David to remain loyal when he was with them hiding from Saul) - 1 Samuel 29:1-7
39. Weak faith of a friend God wishes to bless – 2 Kings 13:14-19
40. Restoration of Jerusalem – (Sanballat was angry with the Jews for rebuilding the wall of Jerusalem.) - Nehemiah 4:1-8
41. Perceived treason – (Jeremiah was imprisoned because he prophesied in favor of the Chaldeans) – Jeremiah 37:11 15

42. Being mocked – (Herod was angry when the wise did not return) - Matthew 2:3,7-9,12,16

43. Ingratitude – The lord was angry because in receiving a kindness, the debtor should have given a kindness.) - Matthew 18:23-35

44. Switched blessings – (Jacob gave Manasseh and Ephraim each other's blessing) - Genesis 48:13-20

45. Forsaking God in favor of man (a king) – The people wanted to be ruled by a man in lieu of God) - 1 Samuel 8:1-9

46. Unjust judgment (seemingly) – (David was displeased because God had slain Uzzah) – 2 Samuel 6:1-11; 1Chronicles 13:1-14

47. Judgment received from God – 1 Kings 20

48. Jesus receiving praise from the people – Matthew 21:14-16

49. Stopping children from seeing Jesus – Mark 10:13-16

50. Self-Importance – Matthew 20:20-28; Mark 10:35-45

51. Sacrificing to Molech – (The king of Moab sacrificed his son (the next in line to the throne) to Molech because they were losing.) - 2 Kings 3

52. Wasting money – Matthew 26:6-13; Mark 14:3-9; John 12:1-8

53. Loss of status or position – Acts 5:12-18

54. The arrest of Jesus – Matthew 26:51; Mark 14:47; Luke 22:50; John 18:2-11

55. Deception revealed – (Peter denied knowing Jesus) - Matthew0 26:57-74; Mark 14:53-71; Luke 22:54-60; John 18:15-18,25-27

56. Heresy – (Saul (Paul) killed and arrested many of the disciples of Jesus - Acts 8:3; 9:1,2; 21:27-31; 23:12-15

57. Lack of perseverance – Acts 12:12; 15:39

# INDEX